Advance Praise

Pritha Gopalan's well-written and carefully researched work makes an important and timely contribution to resolving the impasse in debates about private versus public provision in education. Her smart and detailed empirical analysis of public–private partnerships around the globe makes clear the important differences between "privatization" and "partnership," while providing an astute conceptual framework for identifying key dimensions in, as well as understanding challenges to, successful PPP educational change processes. Policymakers, researchers, and students who are serious about understanding the potential and complexity of public–private partnerships in school change efforts internationally will find this book fascinating and immensely useful.

—Kathleen D. Hall
Associate Professor of Education and Anthropology,
University of Pennsylvania, USA

The book deals comprehensively and lucidly with the complex issue of PPP, a model projected universally as an innovative development strategy. Will quality get diluted when scaling up? Is it feasible to blend private entrepreneurship with public service mindedness? Such complex and delicate questions have been deftly handled. The author's arguments are ably supported by her in depth case studies. The book throws light on the various dimensions of PPP, and is a valuable guide for planners, policymakers, and implementers.

—M. P. Vijayakumar
Member, National Resource Group, Ministry of Human
Resource Development, Government of India and
Member, Southern Regional Council, National Council
for Teacher Education, Ministry of Human Resource
Development, Government of India

Gopalan's thorough examination of PPPs in education is timely and insightful both for the societies where her case studies come from, as well as for those where PPPs are heralded as either panacea or ruination. Through in depth analysis of exemplar cases in the US and India, *PPP Paradox* thus takes us to a superior level in understanding and evaluating PPPs in education past, present, and future.

—**Pedro M. Garcez**
Associate Professor, Federal University of Rio Grande doSul and Fellow, National Council of Scientific and Technological Development, Brazil

PPP PARADOX

Thank you for choosing a SAGE product! If you have any comment, observation or feedback, I would like to personally hear from you. Please write to me at <u>contactceo@sagepub.in</u>

—Vivek Mehra, Managing Director and CEO,
SAGE Publications India Pvt Ltd, New Delhi

Bulk Sales

SAGE India offers special discounts for purchase of books in bulk. We also make available special imprints and excerpts from our books on demand.

For orders and enquiries, write to us at

Marketing Department
SAGE Publications India Pvt Ltd
B1/I-1, Mohan Cooperative Industrial Area
Mathura Road, Post Bag 7
New Delhi 110044, India
E-mail us at <u>marketing@sagepub.in</u>

Get to know more about SAGE, be invited to SAGE events, get on our mailing list. Write today to <u>marketing@sagepub.in</u>

This book is also available as an e-book.

PPP PARADOX

Promise and Perils of Public–Private Partnership in Education

Pritha Gopalan

SAGE www.sagepublications.com
Los Angeles • London • New Delhi • Singapore • Washington DC

First published in 2013 by

SAGE Publications India Pvt Ltd
B1/I-1 Mohan Cooperative Industrial Area
Mathura Road, New Delhi 110 044, India
www.sagepub.in

SAGE Publications Inc
2455 Teller Road
Thousand Oaks, California 91320, USA

SAGE Publications Ltd
1 Oliver's Yard, 55 City Road
London EC1Y 1SP, United Kingdom

SAGE Publications Asia-Pacific Pte Ltd
33 Pekin Street
#02-01 Far East Square
Singapore 048763

Published by Vivek Mehra for SAGE Publications India Pvt. Ltd, Phototypeset in 10/12pt Times New Roman by Diligent Typesetter, Delhi and printed at De-Unique, New Delhi.

Library of Congress Cataloging-in-Publication Data
Gopalan, Pritha.
  PPP paradox : promise and perils of public-private partnership in education / Pritha Gopalan.
      pages cm
  Includes bibliographical references and index.
  1. Privatization in education. 2. Public schools. 3. Education and state.
  4. Educational change. 5. Privatization in education—Michigan—Case studies. 6. Privatization in education—India—Chennai—Case studies. I. Title.
  LB2806.36.G69   379.3—dc23   2013   2013021010

ISBN: 978-81-321-1128-3 (HB)

The SAGE Team: Sutapa Ghosh, Shreya Lall, Nand Kumar Jha, and Rajinder Kaur

Contents

Abbreviations

ABL	Activity-based Learning
AED	Academy for Educational Development
ALM	Active Learning Methodology
AMI	Association Montessori Internationale
AYP	Adequate Yearly Progress
CCSI	Coalition for Comprehensive School Improvement
CMT-C	Center for Montessori Training—Chennai
CMU	Central Michigan University
CREDO	Center for Research on Education Outcomes
CSR	Comprehensive School Reform
CSRD	Comprehensive School Reform Demonstration
DIET	District Institutes of Education and Training
DPEP	District Primary Education Program
EMES	Emergence of Social Enterprise in Europe
EMO	Educational Management Organization
EMU	Eastern Michigan University
EPL	Exercises of Practical Life
ESEA	Elementary and Secondary Education Act
FAO	Food and Agriculture Organization of the United Nations
IAS	Indian Administrative Service
IHE	Institutions of Higher Education
IMA	Indian Montessori Association
IMC	Indian Montessori Center
IPM	Integrated Pest Management
J-PAL	Abdul Jameel Latif Poverty Action Lab
KFI	Krishnamurti Foundation India
LEA	Local Education Agency
MCES	Michigan Coalition of Essential Schools
MMSP	Michigan Middle Start Partnership
NCERT	National Center for Education Research and Testing
NCLB	No Child Left Behind Act
NGO	Nongovernmental Organizations
NMU	Northern Michigan University
NSDC	National Staff Development Council
OMS	Owen Middle School

PISA   Program for International Student Assessment
PPP   Public–Private Partnership
PR-MSP   Puerto Rico Math and Science Partnership
PSP   Public Social Partnerships
OECD   Organization for Economic Cooperation and Development
REAL   Rural Ecology and Agricultural Livelihoods
RTE   Right to Education Act
SEA   State Educational Agency
SRC   School Reform Commission
SRCT   Sri Ramacharan Charitable Trust
SSA   Sarva Shiksha Abhiyan
TEF   Thai Education Foundation
TFA   Teach for All
WDR   World Development Report
WKKF   W. K. Kellogg Foundation

Foreword

This is a wise and thoughtful book that is realistically hopeful. It proposes that for fundamental and enduring change to take place in public schools, a variety of kinds of assistance to school systems from outside partners is necessary. I must say that when I began to read the manuscript I thought, "Necessary? Very helpful, maybe. But to make the argument that outside partnerships are a necessary condition for public school change is a very tall order indeed." However, as I finished reading the manuscript, the author had persuaded me, because she presents a very strong case for her claim.

Mass provision of public schooling has only been in existence for about a century and three quarters. That is just an eyeblinking time: the most recent moment across the entire course of human history and prehistory. Small wonder that we have not yet figured out how to accomplish teaching and learning for almost all students in schools—doing that as well as we do the teaching and learning of walking and talking with almost all children in families. And not surprisingly, parents, other stakeholders, and social critics recognize that public schools do not actually achieve what they espouse as their aim—their putative raison d'être—which is to provide learning opportunity equitably for all their students, a level playing field for learning.

Over the past 175 years there have been repeated calls for public school reform and repeated attempts at it. Often what results is the surface appearance of change rather than reform that is more thorough and enduring—deep change that actually improves the provision of learning opportunity for a wide range of students. Fads for change come and go. Meanwhile, daily life in classrooms and fundamental assumptions and practices in pedagogy continue on much as they have done in the past.

Why is basic school change so elusive? One reason may be that the fads (often nowadays called "treatments" by analogy with medicine) require basic changes in everyday practices if they are to be fully implemented, basic changes in primary service provision by teachers—the school organization's frontline service providers. Unlike particular medicines and surgical procedures, educational "treatments" are not most appropriately conceived as unitary entities that can be considered to be the same phenomenon in instantiation from one time and place to the next, nor do school changes result automatically from the anonymous workings of market forces. (This is why "high fidelity implementation" and "scaling up" are wrong-headed metaphors for school improvement and why "high stakes" accountability procedures by themselves are insufficient to foster fundamental change.) Rather, *learning environments are best conceived as ways of life*, locally constructed by actual people in local communities of practice, involving multidimensional aspects of socially organized interaction, in recurring and mutually influencing acts of communication and interpretation that are continually taking place in real time among teachers, learners, and learning materials. These ways of life are more like gardening than they are like industrial agriculture. Each separate learning environment must be grown anew each year, classroom by classroom, as a set of teaching and learning practices that are situated within distinct local circumstances.

Moreover, it is hard to change a customary way of life—one whose organization is so habitual as to be largely invisible to those who are living it. And teaching is a lonely profession, done in cottage industry circumstances for the most part. As a teacher in a conventional school you close the classroom door and hope for the best, teaching as you yourself were taught. If you as a teacher have never seen or experienced fundamentally different teaching practices, if you have never seen the full upper reach of what your students are actually capable of attaining, intellectually and in their social relationships with one another and with you as their teacher, it is very difficult to change your practice—even to try to change. That would be like jumping off a diving board for the first time; embarking on a voyage across uncharted waters. One is more likely to take a leap into the unknown if one has company in that attempt—the fellowship of those who have taken a similar leap before— friendly critics as partners and guides along a new way.

And as a public school system, its organization as a bureaucracy can increase efficiency to some extent, by setting clear guidelines for a division of labor and for the exercise of authority, thus reducing the inefficiency of corruption. But bureaucratic human service organizations as a social form, by their very commitment to the standard operating procedures that make for organizational coherence, also militate against innovation by trying repeatedly to limit the discretionary authority of their frontline service providers. The paradox is that teachers within school systems need "wiggle room" to grow their own classroom learning environments in local adaptations. That's not corruption, it is opportunity for serendipity. Yet school systems as bureaucracies inhibit teachers' wiggle room, whether as an intended or an unintended consequence of the system's routine operation. Consequently, school organizations need partners at the institutional level—critical friends to help them initiate and sustain more flexible arrangements in the ways they provide resources to classrooms and monitor them—just as individual teachers need partnering in undertaking and sustaining fundamental change in teaching and learning practices at the classroom level, in face-to-face relations with their students. This is labor-intensive work. It takes continuous effort sustained over time. No capital-intensive shortcuts as quick fixes. No silver bullets.

This book shows us clearly how multiple aspects and levels of organization and multiple stakeholders can work together in affecting genuine school change. In the masterful opening chapters of the book, the author presents a comprehensive and nuanced review of recent literature on educational reform and school change, including cross-national examples. This broad and even-handed survey of a variety of policy positions is followed by specific accounts of reform efforts in two case studies, one from a public–private partnership in middle school change in curriculum and instruction that took place in the state of Michigan in the United States, and one from a partnership to bring Montessori education to government-run schools in Chennai, a large Indian city.

Thorough educational change involves basic restructuring of the technology and conduct of everyday routines in teaching and learning interaction. In the Michigan case, these changes involved not only innovations in curriculum but also rearrangements of students' daily work with each other, as they became engaged in project-based learning. Teachers also began to work together in new ways, collaborating across classrooms that were no longer as isolated as they had been before. In the Chennai case, the introduction of Montessori learning materials, with a pedagogical focus on attentionally close engagement with those materials by individual children, resulted in basic changes in the moment-by-moment conduct of student work and of teacher–student relationships in kindergarten classrooms. Specific description in the case studies shows that these changes in the ecology of classroom learning environments were not just superficial, but were fundamental. In its concluding chapter, the book returns to a wide-angle view, summarizing the major points illustrated in the case studies and drawing conclusions for policy in affecting enduring school change.

As you read this book I think you will be persuaded by its argument, as I was. You will come to appreciate the importance of outside-school partnerships in the process of school improvement and you will develop richer understanding of the painstaking, labor-intensive change processes by which genuine educational reform can be initiated and sustained.

Frederick Erickson
Inaugural George F. Kneller Professor of
Anthropology of Education, Emeritus
University of California, Los Angeles

Acknowledgments

It takes a village to write a book, or so it felt over the last few years. I feel fortunate to have had so much support throughout this project.

The ICICI Foundation, Mumbai, India, sponsored my research from October 2008 to September 2010, and I am deeply grateful for their support of my work.

The team at SAGE was extremely responsive and a pleasure to work with. I thank them for the opportunity to publish with SAGE.

I thank Chetana Sabnis and Sneha A., my students at the Indian Institute for Technology Madras, Chennai, for their research and editorial assistance. Their enthusiasm and hard work made the final stretch easier.

My heartfelt gratitude to Leah Meyer Austin, Patrick Montesano, Alexandra (Sandy) Weinbaum, Dick Corbett, Bruce Wilson, Steve Hoelscher, Teri West, Patricia Jessup, and Aurelia Enache, with whom I worked closely on Middle Start. The "Middle Start years," as I think of them, have greatly enriched me professionally and personally. I especially thank Dr Sandy Weinbaum for her valuable comments on the book.

Kalvi Trust, Sri Ramacharan Charitable Trust, Uma Shankar, Padmini Gopalan, and Chitra Mani in Chennai, India, inspired me to start a new study at a time when both my children were toddlers! Nithya Kalyani, a teacher, and true believer in the Montessori project in Chennai, helped me understand the nuances of the method. I thank them for the opportunity to play storyteller to this unique initiative.

I thank Dr Nachiket Mor for the opportunity to deeply engage with the Indian education landscape through my work at the Institute of Financial and Managerial Research.

I thank Dr Frederick Erickson, my mentor from my days as a doctoral student at the University of Pennsylvania, Philadelphia, United States, whose exemplary guidance has stood me in good stead throughout my career.

Where would I be without my lively friends? I know that they will be the first to celebrate this book. I thank Dr Raina Anand for making me see the lighter side of almost everything, and Vidhya Muthuram for helping in so many ways, throughout this process.

My family! I thank my parents Saraswathy and Gopal for their constant love and encouragement. I thank my sister Priya, and Ram and Karun for being a second home for my kids.

This book is for my husband Ramesh, and my sons Manu and Amrith, who ensured that there was enough noise and cheer in our house after my long hours with the computer. My now ten-year-old Manu often asked: "Amma, this book is taking hours and hours. When will it be done?" It's done, Manu.

Introduction

There are important differences between "privatization" and "partnership" that I hope I can make crystal clear through this book. The growing privatization movement in education alarms me, and I hope through this volume to show that ailing public systems, rather than being written off as inefficient and outdated, can be revitalized through partnerships. Yes, there is ample proof that public systems are ailing, and there are a slew of reasons why parents, policymakers, entrepreneurs, and researchers alike are supporting school choice movements all over the world. However, the existing research on various modes of decentralization and privatization is not conclusive, and it is not clear that privatization is a one-size-fits-all solution on a national basis, or that it sufficiently addresses the issue of social equity.

Social equity is the foremost reason why most democracies in the world have public schools and systems. Most public school systems have existed since nations formalized their constitutional identity. Most democracies place education high in their list of national priorities, and several countries make primary schooling compulsory, as education has long been considered critical for human development, socialization, and economic development. However, the long history and sheer size of public education systems, in many cases, have burdened them with heavy bureaucracies, multiple policy streams, shortages of funds and teachers, and increasing enrolment. Structural challenges have hampered the morale of educators and clouded their commitment and focus on teaching and learning. Even staunch advocates of public education will admit that public systems in many parts of the world are not currently fulfilling their obligations.

Similar issues of size, complexity, and questions of efficiency plague other public systems. Execution of other "public" functions such as collecting taxes, conducting elections, maintaining law and order, providing public transport, and managing waste is also complex, and many governments struggle to maintain consistency and quality in these functions. Can we then conclude that all public systems are open for privatization? Clearly there is no scope for decentralization of some of the aforementioned functions. Specifically, running an election or collecting taxes requires a public entity with adequate regulation, a national network, and a focus on the national interest to carry out the task.

Apart from the public mission aspect, it is possible that a private enterprise, if entrusted with a similar scale and scope of work, may become overburdened and inefficient. It is also possible that the same enterprise may decide midway to abandon the project because of employee turnover or financial constraints. In this case, taxes will not be collected and elections not conducted, resulting in national crises. We must first examine the concept of privatization, and its implications for the delivery of certain essential services in a country before we can take sides in the "public vs. private" argument.

Simply put, privatization means decentralizing a public function, and through a contract or other arrangement handing it, either partially or wholly, to a private entity. The reasons for privatizing a function usually have to do with the greater operational efficiencies and productivity of private entities, as compared to public ones. Usually, such benefits are brought about in private entities through the use of technology and modern management systems. Private entities are thought to have faster decision-making processes, flexibility, and responsiveness that help it mitigate emergent problems. They achieve cost-efficiency through streamlined supply chains, a productive workforce, and low overhead. While I am not a financial or managerial expert, I have learned enough about the discourse of privatization to understand that this, in a nutshell, is why privatization is considered an efficient alternative for the delivery of public services.

However, privatization must first be carried out on a national scale for us to see whether *it* can function without the heavy bureaucracies, resource shortages, and policy changes that have undermined the functioning of public systems over time. Its efficiency is not yet proven on the scale at which public systems need to function. Furthermore, remote regions, regions with poor infrastructure, and economically disadvantaged groups that cannot pay for services may be bypassed by a private enterprise if they threaten to bloat costs and/or diminish profits. The pursuit of efficiency through privatization may have harmful effects, which are at least as serious as the current problems we face with inefficiency in public systems. If education is a right that every citizen in a country is entitled to, the pursuit of efficiency may well conflict with equitable delivery if education is entrusted in private hands. Why are we not discussing privatization in conducting elections or tax collection? Mass privatization of public education is just as preposterous.

To resolve the impasse, I propose a solution in the guise of the public–private partnership (PPP) with the important caveat that, in education, such a partnership ensures that the ideals of education quality and equity are not compromised. In this book, I argue that such partnerships can lessen the burden on governments and share the work of updating and sustaining public education systems, provided there are adequate frameworks in place to ensure that the social/public nature of the work is not threatened.

There are already several books and articles on the topic of PPPs in education, which I have referenced throughout this book. Some writers I came across are public policy experts, some are economists, and others are representatives of educational organizations involved in PPPs. I learned a great deal about the history, structure, financing, ethical dilemmas and other facets of PPPs in education. However, it was the rare piece that revealed what a PPP looks like from the inside. Few answered the questions of what really changes for public or government-run schools, and their teachers and students within the context of a PPP, and how such changes take place.

I use the word "change" instead of "improvement," as there can be no unidirectional trajectory for any large-scale effort to improve education systems. Trial and error and ups and downs always characterize education reform. Close, ethnographic research on these important processes can reveal useful patterns of what really works, and how and why it works. The lessons learned from field research can help reformers conceptualize next steps, and solve mid-course challenges. Such documentation of large-scale systemic change can also provide governments, funding organizations, and education reformers with clearer frameworks for new initiatives. One size certainly does not fit all, but careful documentation and distillation of lessons learned from one system can be invaluable for similar efforts in other systems.

While I argue for the PPP, I maintain a critical stance throughout the book, and am careful to enumerate the pitfalls and challenges that line the path of partnerships in education. It is not prudent to look for simple solutions to the complex problem of providing good and equitable public education. However, in the case of PPPs, I argue that the promise outweighs the perils, and buttress my case through integrating primary ethnographic research on two reform initiatives, as well as secondary research that represents a swathe of the education reform literature from different countries.[1]

The paradox, which gives a somewhat prosaic title an intriguing lilt, is contained in this question: What do we need to guard for when private entities work in public, socially relevant, educational spaces? In

Chapter 1, I introduce the paradox, which may occur when the lines between public and private blur. In Chapter 2, I present an original typology of PPPs, based on extensive secondary research: I have inductively arrived at four interacting factors: scope, scale, method, and motive, that when aligned properly can bring about systemic, large-scale, collaborative, socially beneficial improvement. I analyze cases where partnerships have significantly improved curriculum and instruction and greatly engaged students in their learning. Such partnerships have won over teachers from established ways of teaching to fundamentally rethinking what education means, using varied teaching practices, and assuming leadership in refining and sustaining good teaching in their schools and regions. Conversely, I also present cases in which public education systems were compromised by their engagement with partners whose measures did not address improving teaching and learning, but instead focused on control and profitability. Thus, the PPP is no magic bullet, and its capacity for contradictory interpretations needs to be resolved. The four elements of scope, scale, method, and motive help us parse PPPs in education to understand if the approach is of good quality, has reach and builds in sustainability, is collaborative, and if the motive is aligned with the goals of public education.

Chapters 3 and 4 offer detailed, ethnographic case studies of partnerships that truly focused on teaching and learning, and enjoyed a measure of success in actually improving these areas within public systems. Chapter 3 also discusses the importance of an infrastructure that houses the partnership, allowing it to scale up and sustain, throughout a system. Chapter 4 raises concerns about the limitations of partnerships, which though very successful in raising the teaching and learning standards in pilot schools, are less able to take on the challenge of system-wide infusion in a timely manner. This arises from the nuanced nature of educational reform and the need for reformers to focus on building systems that support scale-up, even as they focus on improving the quality of teaching and learning at the classroom level. The ethnographic case studies are evidence of the promise of PPPs where scope, method, and motive come together to significantly improve educational systems. The cases also demonstrate the challenges of scaling up and sustaining initiatives in the long term, as scale requires private and public partners to have adequate human and financial resources, and a supportive policy climate to grow their work.

Chapter 5 closes the book by bringing together the issues of scope, scale, method, and motive and ponders whether the model of the social enterprise is a good fit for PPPs in education. The chapter synthesizes key points in the emerging literature on Public Social Partnerships (PSP), including their history, purposes, areas of work, and monitoring mechanisms. The leaders in this area are some of the countries within the European Union, which floated PSPs as a means of retaining the public and social emphasis of their services, while blending it with an entrepreneurial approach that allowed private partners to scale up and sustain their work.

Anthropologists hold that the researchers' subjective experiences are inextricably intertwined with the lens with which they view society. Even as I passionately argued the cause of public education in this book, I was acutely aware that I was the beneficiary of a great private education, and that my children are in the best private school that I can afford to send them to. My children changed three schools (all private) before we settled on a fourth that met all my expectations, a direct product of my preoccupation with educational quality. Thus, a school by nature of being "private" does not automatically become "good." A good school needs, at its core, good teaching and engaged learning. There are volumes of educational literature devoted to the challenges to improving teaching and learning. A mere takeover of public education by private entities will not diminish these challenges, unless it is focused on understanding why such challenges exist, and what will help resolve them.

All parents, rich and poor, share an aspiration to put their children in a "good" school. Cost, quality, and distance are three important criteria that parents typically consider when judging schools. Vibrant public education systems are critical for those parents and children who do not have the option of paying for a great school, or traveling long distances to attend one. Vibrant public systems meet the dual obligations of educational access and quality that are constitutional rights in many democracies. Simply moving children from low-income families from a poor public school to a poor private one does not, in any way, fulfill their right to education.

The "fortune at the bottom of the pyramid" is a huge one in education, as lower-income families in developing countries typically have many children, and believe that education guarantees a brighter future for them. Low-fee private schools are springing up in several parts of rural and suburban India, and in similar regions of other developing countries, to offer such families local educational options. However, low-fee private schools may also be low on educational quality. Proponents of private education for the poor hold that there are shining examples of low-fee schools in some regions that offer a viable and academically effective alternative to local state-run schools.[2] Opponents maintain that their claims are overstated, and that most low-fee schools employ teachers with little or no preparation, turn away those who cannot pay, and have inadequate infrastructure and overcrowded classrooms. Some also caution that low-fee private schools may be purely profit-making enterprises, or may promote a particular religion or ideology.[3] We will be back in the proverbial square one, if the result of a large private takeover of public education is similar in quality to the average low-fee private school.

There is no clear, large-scale alternative yet to public education. Through this book I urge educational thinkers, activists, foundations, policymakers, and government authorities to seriously consider the PPP, more specifically the PSP, as a viable alternative that will revitalize public education.

PPPs have been in use for a long time, and in many countries, to build roads and bridges, clean rivers, and manage waste. In the last two decades, they have slowly begun to make their presence felt in the field of public education. Several countries, including the United States and India, have even enacted laws that include partnerships with private entities as a vehicle for education reform. This book acknowledges that trend and seeks to contribute to the body of literature emerging on PPPs in education, with the important difference that it seeks to understand different types of PPPs, and the implications for educational quality, scale, and sustainability within each type.

NOTES

1. Due to the varying national origins of the literature cited, both American and British English spellings and usage are reflected in the cited portions of this book.
2. See Tooley (2009) and Tooley, Dixon, and Gomathi (2007) for a discussion of the contributions of low-fee private schools. See Sarangapani and Winch (2010) for a critique of Tooley et al. (2007).
3. See Akaguri (2011) and Lewin and Little (2011) for critiques of low-fee private schools on the basis of their quality, enrollment practices, and student achievement.

1

The Paradox

With all that we know now about education, it is clear that public education is an essential service, and that it is crying out for improvement in developing and developed countries alike. It is also clear that while public education needs to remain public, it needs partners outside the government to keep it up-to-date, efficient, transparent, and engaging. Therein lies a contradiction, as with the entry of partners, the lines between public and private begin to blur, and the genre of the PPP opens itself to use and misuse, depending on the nature and intent of the partners. The need for partners and reform arises from the difficult and complex task of providing good education, which is good teaching and engaged learning, in huge public systems. In Chapter 2, I present my typology of PPPs according to whether their scope is focused or systemic; scale is experimental or policy-driven; method is top-down as in a takeover, or complementary; and motive is profit or social. The paradox arises when the scope, scale, method, and/or motive of a partnership are subverted to serve causes other than educational improvement. I, for example, would view a focused, policy-driven, takeover, for-profit initiative as completely contrary to the goals and purposes of public education. I would view a systemic, policy-driven, complementary, social initiative as holding great promise for the improvement of teaching and learning. I hope that you see my point of view after reading this book, as historically education is inextricably tied to human and social development.

I was involved in two different efforts by public and private entities to jointly improve large educational systems. In both cases, partners were focused on improving teaching and learning in a long-term, sustained manner with the aim of reducing social inequalities. I believe these stories are important, as they were working on a core service, public education, and trying to add value to existing systems through partnership. Several countries have long had public systems of education, and have institutionalized these systems early in their sociopolitical development, as educators, philosophers, social thinkers, and politicians have continuously emphasized the importance of formal education in building a country's technical and cultural capital. Thomas Jefferson, the third President of the United States famously said (Jefferson, 1806):

> *Education is here placed among the articles of public care, not that it would be proposed to take its ordinary branches out of the hands of private enterprise, which manages so much better all the concerns to which it is equal; but a public institution can alone supply those sciences which, though rarely called for, are yet necessary to complete the circle, all the parts of which contribute to the improvement of the country, and some of them to its preservation.*

Tyack and Cuban (1995), reputed historians of American public education, have documented the importance placed on public education in the United States by policy makers and the public alike. They write: "Reforming public schools has long been a favorite way of improving not just education but society. ... For over a century and a half, Americans have translated their cultural anxieties and hopes into dramatic demands for educational reform" (p. 1).

Governments in developed and developing countries alike are mandating that students enroll in schools for a period, usually until they complete secondary education (equivalent to Class 12). In the United States, the period is between 6 to 16 years of age in many states (Education Commission of the States, 2010). In India, it is for a period of 8 years, spanning the ages of 6 to 14 years. According to a recent UNESCO report, India, with the landmark Right to Education Act of 2009, is one of 135 countries that has regulation supporting compulsory education (United Nations Education, Scientific, and Cultural Organization, 2010). Several countries provide free, compulsory education for a minimum duration of 6 years, until the completion of primary school (Jin & Zhang, 2008). Recent entrants in compulsory education are Singapore in 2003 (Ministry of Education—Singapore, 2012) and Pakistan in 2009. The National Education Policy of Pakistan aims at improving access, enrolment, and quality of education in government schools (Ministry of Education—Pakistan, 2009).

Education is viewed as essential for the all-round growth and success of individuals, and hence the important role of the government in ensuring that education is available to those who cannot pay for private schooling. The scope for private participation exists because of the huge need for, and difficulty in, delivering good education. The World Development Report (2004), focused specifically on the issue of delivering services to the poor of the world, takes the stance that governments in developing countries are primarily responsible for the delivery of health and education, but need to seek the help of other partners for the delivery to meet quality and equity parameters. The World Development Report (WDR) states:

> *By financing, providing, or regulating the services that contribute to health and education outcomes, governments around the world demonstrate their responsibility for the health and education of their people. Why? First, these services are replete with market failures—with externalities, as when an infected child spreads a disease to playmates or a farmer benefits from a neighbor's ability to read. So the private sector, left to its devices, will not achieve the level of health and education that society desires. Second, basic health and basic education are considered fundamental human rights. The Universal Declaration of Human Rights asserts an individual's right to "a standard of living adequate for the health and well-being of himself and of his family, including ... medical care ... [and a right to education that is] ... free, at least in the elementary and fundamental stages." No matter how daunting the problems of delivery may be, the public sector cannot walk away from health and education. The challenge is to see how the government—in collaboration with the private sector, communities, and outside partners—can meet this fundamental responsibility. (p. 3)*

The private sector, in much writing on PPPs, does not just imply private enterprises or nonprofit organizations, as is commonly understood. Several writers see private participation as including local communities as they best understand the context in which their schools operate, and have a strong interest in improving them. Stone, Henig, Jones, and Pierannunzi (2001), political scientists who look at the relationships between civic capacity and the quality of education, write: "Local initiatives, sustained by local coalitions, must generate the capacity to get things started and draw in resources from the outside. ... It is to this that we are referring when we use the term civic capacity." Such civic capacity driving a PPP will root it in the community that it will benefit, and possibly sustain the effort in the long term. Private participation can take the form of coalitions that support educational reform, formed by nongovernmental organizations, parent and community groups, and foundations. Educational partners may be nonprofit organizations, or for-profit companies. Increasingly, there is support for private participation in many countries, as research and best practices have changed rapidly, and beleaguered public systems are seen as more efficiently improving their capacity (in qualitative and quantitative terms) with help from outside experts.

Patrinos and Sosale (2007), in their edited volume on PPPs in education, represent varied vehicles of partnership such as charter schools, voucher programs, and contracts for instructional and non-instructional services in developed and developing countries. The book reviews available evidence of impact on student achievement, and barriers to and achievements of these PPPs. The book scans different types of partnerships for public education in countries such as Brazil, Colombia, Venezuela, United States, and England. However, there are few descriptive examples of what the schools within these partnerships look like, and what has essentially changed in classrooms, as a result of these initiatives.

LaRocque (2008) lists the following types of programs from an international survey of PPPs in education. He writes:

The private sector has been involved in the delivery of "public" services such as water and transport for many years. However, the extension of PPPs into social policy areas such as health and education is more recent and is arguably one of the most significant trends in public finance in the past decade. ...There is a wide range of PPPs in use in the Basic Education sector each with different characteristics, design features and country contexts. ... PPPs can be classified into seven categories:

- Private sector philanthropic initiatives;
- School management initiatives, under which educational agencies contract directly with private providers to operate public schools or manage certain aspects of public school operations. Although these schools are privately managed, they remain publicly owned and funded;
- Government purchase initiatives under which governments contract with private schools to deliver education at public expense;

- Voucher and voucher-like initiatives under which governments fund students to attend private schools;
- Adopt-a-school programs under which private sector partners provide cash and in-kind resources to complement government funding of public schools;
- School capacity-building initiatives under which private sector partners provide teacher training and curriculum enhancement programs; and
- School infrastructure initiatives under which private sector partners design, finance, construct and operate public school infrastructure under long-term contracts with the government. (p. 9)

While Patrinos and Sosale (2007) and LaRoque (2008) discuss international examples and a range of formats for PPPs, respectively, they do not differentiate between PPPs that have the potential to revitalize public education, and those that divert students and resources to private schools. Clearly, these two kinds of PPPs have very different orientations and implications. Revitalizing public education through partnership implies that public resources stay within the system, and the partnership works for the betterment of the system. On the other hand, PPPs in which the government hands over resources to private schools in return for students enrolling in the latter imply that the public system will continue to function as before, or be further depleted, as resources are withdrawn to support private schools. This important distinction is also a subject of ideological debates between supporters of public schools and privatization enthusiasts. There are numerous examples of public education systems that have benefited from private participation, and the two cases in this book are examples of the value a good partnership can add to students and teachers' experiences in public schools. However, there are numerous cases of exploitative, misguided, and harmful private participation, some of which I document in detail in Chapter 2.

Intentional and well-designed partnerships in education are relatively recent, and need further observation and study, before we can conclude whether they are useful or not. My experience with two partnerships, both involving reputable nonprofits in alliances with public authorities showed much promise, hence my argument in favor of such partnerships, with, of course, limits on scope, method, and motive. Both partnerships built their capacity over time to qualitatively improve teaching and learning, slowly infuse good practices throughout systems, and grow from a pilot to larger-scale effort.

The emerging literature on PSP is relevant in this context, and I have summarized essential aspects of it in the concluding section of this book. This still-small body of literature focuses on partnerships seeking to improve delivery of public services, especially in the European Union, through clearly specified roles and activities arrived at collaboratively between the public and the "third" or not-for-profit sectors. A few pilots conducted in Italy, Scotland, Ireland, Poland, and other European countries show promise in improving services, with a firm focus on the "social" or "public" aspect of the work. The choice of "private" partners has been limited in these pilots to those that have a record of working in the voluntary and nonprofit sector, and work strictly in the public interest. PSPs are closely linked with social enterprises, the literature on which is extensive, and documents several efforts in Europe that have successfully bridged the public–private issue by creating an identity that is social and entrepreneurial at the same time, but not motivated by profit or self-interest. I discuss pertinent aspects of this literature, although unfortunately there are no examples of PSPs operating on a large scale in educational reform.

There is a huge unresolved issue confronting those in education reform—"the question of measurement." In Chapter 2, the section on remedial or focused education as one entry point for a partnership shows that it is relatively easy to measure outcomes in such a venture, even to randomize and pinpoint a causal effect. However, in systemic reform, comprehensive school reform, and the multitude of other approaches, which take a multifaceted look at educational problems and attempt long-term, multilayered solutions, causality remains a question. Therefore, when I say that one or the other approach is "promising" or "adds value," it is from a qualitative angle, using educational indices that encompass the quality of teaching, learning, the reach and buy-in that the initiative garners, its ability to scale up with a school district or region, and its capacity to root in a system so that its promise sustains past the initial period of engagement. Wherever possible, I have included outcome data from standardized assessments and other quantitative tests of student achievement. In some cases there are competing accounts, where one group of researchers may find gains and another group a static or even downward trend in achievement. It may be best to view student outcomes as one aspect of an initiative at a particular point in time, and consult all available data on a project to assess the value it adds to teaching and learning.

Most large-scale reforms are documented by internal as well as external researchers and evaluators. One can come to some conclusions about promise or value only from taking a long-term and consolidated look at the body of work on an initiative, and even then only arrive at a subjective judgment. Newer approaches such as value-added research, mixed methods approaches, and multi-sited ethnography are meeting the needs of these increasingly complex initiatives. I have attempted to look widely at the research available on the different approaches discussed in this chapter, and present a fair picture of whether or not they add value.

I came across a thoughtful piece on the meanings and roles of testing in education in the World Development Report (2004). It is a sign of the times that an organization heavy with economists and statisticians takes a questioning view, as few interventions have changed the essential features of schooling despite decades of effort and low achievement continues to plague developing and developed countries alike. The report states:

Schooling has multiple outputs—some easily assessed others not. Assessing mastery of simple skills through standardized testing is fairly straightforward. But it is difficult to assess how well schooling has conveyed a conceptual mastery that allows application to real-world problems. It is still more difficult to assess how well schooling has encouraged creativity. And it is even more difficult to assess how well schooling has conveyed values. Assessing success is further complicated because different actors assign different values to different objectives. Designing an accountability system is difficult because it is difficult to attribute specific outcomes—or even outputs—to specific actors. If a 15-year-old has mastered algebraic concepts, who deserves credit and in what proportion? The parents' genes? The child's nutrition? The parents' motivation and efforts? The child's peers? The child's primary school math teachers? Another teacher who motivated the child to do well in all subjects? The child's current algebra teacher? Nearly all empirical studies of measured learning achievement agree that home background accounts for most of the explainable variation in learning outcomes, especially in primary grades. The same studies disagree widely about how much can be attributed to a child's school. The recent Programme for International Student Assessment study found wide variation in differences in student performance within or between schools. ... Half or more of the variation in performance across schools was

due to variation in students' socioeconomic status, not to factors
under school control. In poorer countries the effect of schools is
larger—and that of parental background smaller. But, in general,
identifying the school's value added is not simple. Even for outputs
easier to specify and measure, not much is known about how
inputs affect them. Economists summarize this relationship under
the metaphor of a "production function." Little is known about
this function because instruction involves human beings—teachers
and students—in all their complexity. For instance, there is ongo-
ing, vigorous debate about the relevance of class size for student
test scores. Some assert that class size is irrelevant, or nearly so.
Some assert that reductions in class size have such a salutary
impact on performance that they are a cost-effective means of
improving performance. After more than a century of widespread
use of classroom instruction, intelligent, well-meaning, and
methodologically sophisticated researchers are still debating
such a seemingly simple issue. That shows how truly complex the
research questions are—the results will vary across time, content,
and context." (pp. 118–119)

The passage from the WDR does a remarkable job of synthesizing the challenges inherent in defining learning, measuring it, attributing improvements in learning to particular causes, and pushing for education research and testing to address this complexity. However, few researchers have taken up this challenge, as much writing on educational outcomes is still about standardized testing. Several writers on the topic of PPPs in education cite a cross-country study of educational outcomes by Woessmann (2006). This paper studies correlations between variables of public–private financing and public–private operation, and their effect on student's cognitive skills on an international test of mathematics, science, and reading. Woessmann's analysis indicates that public funding with private operation of public schools is correlated with better student performance: He writes: "Across countries, public operation of schools is negatively associated with student performance in math, reading and science, while public funding of schools is positively associated with student performance in the three subjects." He finds PPPs where the state finances schools but contracts their operation out to the private sector are very effective. PPPs that require private funding but keep the operation of schools with the public sector fare the worst. He concludes: "Thus, the results favor the particular form of educational PPPs where the state does the funding and the private sector runs the schools" (Woessmann, 2006, p. 20).

However, Woessmann's analysis is at the country level, and does not discuss differences within countries or any variation within the category of publicly financed and privately operated schools. The results do not account for variations in the socioeconomic background of students, or by whether such schools serve students of different abilities equitably. The study does not consider whether the private operation in question is for-profit or not, and if student achievement varies between these two types. The report is based entirely on statistical analysis, and there is no clear explanation of why this combination of finance and operation is so promising. For instance, does it provide superior curricular or instructional support to teachers? Does it engage students better in their learning? How systemic are the partnerships that were studied? For what lengths of time were they in place? While interesting as a macro study of a complex topic, it leaves many critical questions, such as those raised by WDR (2004), unanswered.

Part of the answer to these questions is provided by a recent report by the Organization for Economic Co-operation and Development (OECD, 2012). This report exhaustively analyzes results from the Program for International Student Assessment (PISA) with a view to understand how social stratification in school systems worldwide affects student achievement. One of the findings is that low levels of social stratification are correlated with higher achievement on PISA. Countries with lower social stratification also had greater public spending going to private schools. The report states that (2012, p. 10): "Parents and students do not have to choose between equity/social cohesion and strong performance in their school systems. The two are not mutually exclusive."

I would urge that these findings must be interpreted carefully, as a wholesale handover of public finances to private schools without adequate regulation and oversight may not necessarily result in equity or achievement. It is significant that most of the countries with high levels of public financing of private schools mentioned in the OECD report are in Western or Eastern Europe, where PPP have played a significant role for a few decades in several areas of governance, and strict regulation is already in place for oversight of such partnerships. The other example in the report is of China–Hong Kong, where again there is strict regulation for most kinds of private enterprise, including private schools. This point about regulation is critical, as private management of public schools is a vast and variegated arena, and adequate controls need to be in place to ensure that it stays focused on reducing social stratification and improving learning and achievement.

Writing on PPPs in education has mushroomed over the years that I spent researching and writing this book. There are strident voices pro and con PPPs in education, and a few analyses of their relationships to student outcomes. These vocal arguments have developed even before we have fully understood the different forms of PPPs, their motives, implications, and challenges. With this book I hope to "deconstruct" this oft-used, but not fully understood term, and present a picture that fully considers its promise and perils. There is great value in taking an *interpretive approach* to the issue and first looking in detail at the types of PPPs and their trajectories over time before coming to a firm conclusion of whether or not we need them in education.

Based on my long-term involvement in two initiatives, the first in the United States, and the second in India, I describe the actual workings of each partnership. The first initiative was a snowball that grew very large over the period of my involvement, and I had the opportunity to watch it successfully grow at very close quarters. This reform effort is "Middle Start," initiated by the W.K. Kellogg Foundation, Academy for Educational Development, and numerous other partners who became involved as it unfolded over 10 years. Middle Start, with its focus on improving underserved, low-performing schools with middle grades is a great case to analyze because it grappled long and hard with the issues of quality of teaching and learning, socially equitable approaches, and attention to scaling and sustaining its promising approach.

The second initiative is the Montessori infusion in Chennai Corporation schools. This joint effort of the Kalvi Trust, Sri Ramacharan Charitable Trust, and the Corporation of Chennai has grown from a one-school project to a multi-school initiative, and would benefit thousands if it went system-wide. This project has brought a tried-and-tested method of early childhood education, usually available only in private schools, to public schools. Although the project is still small in scale, the Montessori Method so captured the imagination of teachers and parents that they have thrown their support behind it and enabled the Corporation and the Trusts to work collaboratively grow the initiative across all Corporation preschools and kindergartens. However, the cost of Montessori materials continues to slow down the spread of the initiative, as each environment needs a dedicated and expensive set of materials, which neither partner can easily afford, in the case of a system-wide implementation.

I am currently based in India where "Sarva Shiksha Abhiyan" (SSA— Education for All) emerged as a major educational policy vehicle paving the way for partnerships between public and private entities. In many cases it enabled local government bodies to enter into partnerships with established educational organizations that helped revamp different aspects of the system, focusing mainly on curriculum and instruction. A section titled "policy-driven partnerships" documents some examples of the kinds of partnerships that have sprung up as part of SSA and early reviews of their work. An excerpt of SSA's stance on private participation is as follows (Ministry of Human Resource Development, n.d.):

PUBLIC–PRIVATE PARTNERSHIP IN SSA

Sarva Shiksha Abhiyan takes note of the fact that provision of elementary education is largely made by the government and government aided schools. ...Government, Local Body, and government aided schools would be covered under the Sarva Shiksha Abhiyan, as is the practice under the Mid Day Meal scheme and DPEP.[1] In case private sector wishes to improve the functioning of a government, local body or a private aided school, efforts to develop a partnership would be made within the broad parameters of State policy in this regard. Depending on the State policies, DIETs[2] and other Government teacher-training institutes could be used to provide resource support to private unaided institutions, if the additional costs are to be met by these private bodies.

Research on SSA's partnerships initiatives is emerging, and this book is firmly located within the fast-changing context of public education reform in India. The recent efforts of the Human Resource Department to institutionalize partnerships with private entities through the new Education Act is very relevant, as it provides for varied degrees of partnership and goes as far as to allow private control of public schools in remote areas. The following is an excerpt from an article by Tilak (2010) on whether or not this will compromise the social aims of education and its implications for the quality of education, especially for students in remote areas. Tilak writes that the plan aims to set up 2,500 schools in remote areas through PPPs which will be run by private entities. According to him:

Each school will have about 2,500 students, 1,000 of whom will be from deprived sections and charged a token fee. ...They will be required to pay a monthly fee of ₹25 each. The rest of the children, who will be from other deprived sections—non-income tax paying families—will be required to pay a fee of ₹50 a month. The remaining costs of these students, estimated to be ₹1,000 to ₹1,200 a head per month, will be reimbursed by the Union government to the schools. It is estimated that the government will have to pay ₹10,500 crore until 2017.

Tilak critiques the following financial arrangements allowed under the plan as detrimental to the goals of public education:

One, it involves a massive transfer of resources from the exchequer to private schools. Two, the schools have unlimited freedom in all aspects of governance, including specifically the fees to be charged from the 1,500 students. The model thus allows the so-called non-profit institutions to work for, and actually make, profits. Third, the government has little control over these schools. Except to insist that 1,000 students from the deprived sections be admitted and that they be charged a certain fee, it cannot do much. ...As a result, the model, which claims that it is not for privatisation, and that it will not allow the profit motive to enter the field of education, will promote the opposite: privatisation and, in practice, a high degree of commercialisation. It is privatisation and commercialisation with a difference—utilising public funds.

The Right to Education Act (RTE), drafted in India in 2009, has also added to fuel to educational debates in the country around the provision mandating that all private schools retain 25 percent of their seats for children from lower-income backgrounds (Jha & Parvathi, 2010). The Supreme Court upheld the constitutional validity of the law in the summer of 2012, just before the 2012–13 academic year began. A portion of government funds that went to paying for free and compulsory schooling in public schools was to be diverted to private schools, although many private educators protested that the per pupil expenditures were too low to meet their operating costs. While it is relatively early to predict the outcome of what many in India have called "social engineering," it is clear that public authorities have at least partially given up on public systems.

Some progressive educators have lauded the Act and seen it as a move that will blur well-entrenched class lines in Indian society. Others, progressive and conservative alike, have raised many cautions, the main one being that there are not enough private schools to accommodate all the students from public schools that may potentially want to move; that a large proportion of private schools perform only marginally better than public schools on several educational criteria; and a 25 percent increase in class size in an already overcrowded private school, without any increases in numbers of teachers or exposure for teachers on how to address a mixed group of students, may prove counterproductive to students from lower- and higher-income families alike (Sankaranarayanan, 2012).

While the RTE quota is a radical piece of legislation and could usher in a new, more equitable era in Indian class relations, it does not, at present, seem promising. News reports mostly state that private schools are against the legislation and rather than ushering in an era of greater equality are actively discriminating against the few students enrolled so far through the RTE quota. A report in the *Deccan Chronicle* (2012) states that despite the Supreme Court upholding the 25 per cent quota in private schools in April 2012, several private schools have ignored the stipulation by claiming that they completed admissions in February 2012, and cannot take in more students in the current academic year.

The most alarming report I have read to date states that children admitted a private school in Bangalore, India, under the 25 percent reservation quota stipulated by RTE were seated in the back rows of classrooms, ignored by their teachers and classmates, and identified by cutting off a lock of their hair on their foreheads (Bangalore Bureau, *Hindu*, 2012). Parents who were interviewed by the reporter said that their children were traumatized by the discrimination they faced from teachers and students, but that their complaints to the school authorities had fallen on deaf ears. The reporter quoted a former minister who termed it a "new form of untouchability."

The act at present does not seem to be supported with an infrastructure of adequate funding, clear guidelines for building the capacity of private educators to meet this challenge, and an equitable system of admission for public school students seeking to make the change to private schools. There are also several news reports of a resource crunch at the Central government, which is supposed to share the costs on a 65:35 basis with state governments (Dhawan, 2012). A few news reports also documented a low level of demand for the free seats, as only a few parents applied for the allotted seats for the 2012–13, and most schools were undersubscribed for the seats set aside (*Times of India*, 2012). Some writers have wondered about how the Indian government will bear the costs of the Sarva Shiksha Abhiyan and Right to Education Act "combine," as the funds available are a little more than half of what it will take to implement the joint scheme to full effect (Kumar, 2012).

The real workings of RTE 2009 will reveal themselves over the next 2 or 3 years. This is an interesting and critical area for a new study. It is clear that the RTE Act is here to stay and that it has the potential to meet some of the unmet needs of lower-income families and students. However, the ailing public system must not be forgotten and a parallel track of investment and effort must work toward its revitalization and expansion to meet the vast and growing demand for education in India. The PPP or specifically the PSP is a real solution that must receive the attention it deserves.

PPPs have succeeded in spawning many experiments in India, the United States, and many other countries. As stated earlier, I identified four types of partnerships through an extensive review of the literature on education reform. In Chapter 2, I analyze them using the lenses of scope, scale, method, and motive.

NOTES

1. District Primary Education Program (DPEP).
2. District Institutes of Education and Training (DIETS) are teacher training institutes at the district level.

2

Promise and Perils

Anthropologists view social phenomena as composed of several intentional and unintentional sets of activities that when knit together produce and reproduce our social world. The way the knit happens is guided by the meanings that people attach, individually and as groups, to their activities. The patterning of these meanings and their evolution over time makes and remakes culture. Looking at social processes as constantly co-created by individuals and groups with varied cultures enables us to expect and understand the multiple manifestations of an idea or action. An inductive approach allows the researcher to gradually understand ideas and actions from the perspectives of several different individuals and groups involved in the activity and discern patterns or groupings in these perspectives and experiences. Such an in-depth representation allows readers of the work to hear actual perspectives of insiders and develop more nuanced understandings of the social activity under discussion.

Bringing the interpretive strength of anthropology to the study of PPP in education is very useful, as a PPP is an intersection point where public meets private, and brings the habits, practices, strengths and challenges of each into close interaction. Public education systems vary by nation, region, the demography they serve, the policy frameworks they operate under, and several other important criteria. Private partners are also equally varied, and criteria such as their motives, areas of work, skills and experience, and ability to scale will influence how they carry out their role. The PPP co-created by a particular set of partners is bound to bring their prior identities into interaction and will evolve a joint identity as well as the work progresses. There is a need to understand these nuances of PPPs, as using "PPP" as an umbrella term does not help us grasp its variations. Some variations may help bring about great improvements in public education, some may prove redundant, and still others may even cause greater dysfunction.

In this chapter, I use an inductive approach to study the research on PPPs from different countries, classify them, and situate the categories in relevant literature on education quality, especially the implications for teaching and learning. Where possible, I also tie the discussion to the literature on student assessment and achievement.

I have identified four critical lenses from which to examine the workings of PPPs. They are as follows:

- Scope: Focused or Systemic
- Scale: Experimental or Policy-driven
- Method: Takeover or Complementary
- Motive: Profit or Social

Scope refers to whether a PPP seeks to improve a specific aspect of education or is a comprehensive approach to addressing systemic problems. *Scale* refers to whether a PPP is a pilot or whether it is a large-scale policy-driven effort. *Method* refers to whether a PPP is top-down or a complementary partnership. *Motive* refers to whether the PPP is motivated by self-interest or is focused on the larger public interest.

Put together, these lenses help us understand PPPs for the quality of education they foster, the scale at which they operate and sustain, the political climate of a PPP, and the goals that drive its work. I use this framework to present cases of educational partnerships from developed and developing countries, including India, Puerto Rico, Thailand, and the United States.

SCOPE: FOCUSED OR SYSTEMIC

Focused Partnerships

Public education systems in many countries have at one time or another worked with partners on focused reform efforts, such as improving reading in the elementary grades or training teachers in a particular curricular and/or instructional method. Such partnerships usually tend to be of a short duration of 1–3 years, have well-defined implementation plans and budgets, and have clear goals and related activities. Focused interventions were the norm earlier in the history of school reform, as educational issues were viewed with the same lens as issues in public health,[1] and short-term interventions such as pull-out programs for slower learners, remedial literacy or numeracy programs, and short-term teacher training courses were common antidotes to low student achievement or to improve particular aspects of teaching. Focused programs are still popular with policy makers as they are short term, scalable, cost-effective, and aim for measurable outcomes. The following example of Pratham's "Balsakhi" program shows how one such focused program operates.

Pratham is a large Indian nonprofit organization, working in various parts of India to improve educational access and quality. Pratham initiated Balsakhi, a remedial education intervention in rural government schools to support struggling students to improve their literacy and numeracy skills. The program employed tutors, or *balsakhis*, usually local women from the same area, who worked with the lowest-performing primary schoolchildren in the class. This program was implemented in 122 public primary schools in Vadodara and 77 schools in Mumbai, and was later expanded to include Delhi. According to a study of the Balsakhi program conducted by Banerjee and his co-researchers at the Abdul Jameel Latif Poverty Action Lab (J-PAL), the *balsakhi* was usually a young woman from the same region as the students who worked with children in grades 2, 3, and 4 who were identified for support services in the area of basic reading and math skills. The *balsakhi* met with a group of 15–20 children for about two hours of the four-hour school day. J-PAL (n.d.) describes the study design as follows:

In the 2001 school year approximately half of the schools were given a tutor for grade 3, and the other half were given a tutor for grade 4—which school received which was randomized. In 2002, the schools were given a tutor for the previously untreated grade. In determining program impact, grade 3 students in schools that had a tutor were compared to grade 3 students at schools that had tutors for grade 4. (p. 1)

Banerjee, Cole, Duflo, and Linden (2005) writing about the results of the randomized evaluation report that the program showed,

...substantial positive impacts on children's academic achievement. Scores on tests administered after the program showed that in both cities in both years, the program improved overall test scores, with the biggest gains in math. The number of students in the bottom third of program classes who passed basic competency tests increased by nearly 8%, while those in the top third who passed increased by 4%. (p.1)

However, the researchers also note that the gains did not sustain at the same rate after the first year. Banerjee et al. (2005) write:

> *On the one hand, the fact that, one year after both programs, those who benefited the most from them are still 0.10 standard deviations ahead of those who did not, is encouraging. ... On the other hand, the rate of decay over these two years is rapid: if the decay continued at this rate, the intervention would very soon have had no lasting impact. ... Perhaps the only way to retain the gains is to constantly reinforce new learning. (p. 15)*

The study also highlights implications for rapid scaling up of this remedial program, which depended only on young women within each locality and could be continued despite rapid turnover among *balsakhi*s. In a policy-oriented article, J-PAL (2006) emphasizes that the program was also very cost-effective as the only cost was the salary of the *balsakhi*s, which was nominal, and the increase in student achievement was substantial, given the low investment.

The writers note that the program was implemented on a large scale in several Indian districts due to its inexpensive and effective approach (Banerjee et al., 2005). While the program is a good illustration of a focused, short-term intervention run in partnership with government systems, it has not been studied over a five-year period or more, and continuing benefits of the program to the children as they go to the next grade and beyond remain unknown.

It is important to state here that focused programs, such as remedial approaches in which children are segregated on the basis of ability, are critiqued extensively by many educationists, as they contribute to ability groupings that have detrimental effects on children's self-perceptions, social interactions, and overall development. Commonly termed "pull-out" programs, such approaches are seen as exacerbating inequalities in places where social and ability differentiation are already deep-rooted. Some researchers, such as Loveless (1999), have shown a positive correlation between grouping students according to ability and student achievement. However, several others point out that remedial education through pull-out programs does not address the reasons why the system fails some children in the first place. Several researchers and reformers have spoken out strongly in favor of sustained involvement in school systems with overall improvement of teaching and learning as the end goal to helping teachers effectively address the needs of students of different learning levels (Oakes, 1986, 2008). Among the solutions proposed, differentiated instruction (Tomlinson, Brimjoin, & Narvaez, 2008) is widely supported by researchers and the teaching community alike and has strong roots in constructivist thinking in education. A detailed discussion of differentiated instruction is outside the scope of this book. Those interested in learning more about this may consult the work of Lev Vygotsky, Howard Gardner, and Carol Ann Tomlinson.

Education reformers also consider short-term remedial programs as "band aid" covering the larger problems that would ne d long-term, comprehensive solutions (Legters, McDill, & McPartland, 1992). Challenges to learning, are situated in the broader context of teaching, school policies, and infrastructure. Bringing in a focused educational intervention masks the larger problem of a school system that cannot accommodate the needs of varied students. Fink (2000), in a book subtitled *Why School Reform Doesn't Last*, writes:

The model of change was simple, straightforward, and linear. Input → Process → Output. ... In addition to its linearity, and the assumption that adoption of an innovation solved all problems, this model presupposed, somewhat arrogantly, that change was something that experts invented and initiated outside the school, and once teachers understood the Inherent wisdom of the change, they would leap at the opportunity to behave as intended... Unfortunately most of the innovations...withered and died. (p. 2)

Aladjem and Borman (2006), meta-analysts of school reform in the United States, write about the trend away from focused programs to whole school solutions:

Local school- and district-based reformers have been assisted by a strikingly large number of federal and state policies that have evolved over the last 40 years. These policies have shifted from targeting individual students for additional assistance through Title I and other similar programs to developing and institutionalizing universal high standards governing teaching and learning for all students, emphasizing schools as the most effective sites for change.

There is wide consensus that the heart of education is teaching and learning, and increasingly the focus is on quality teaching through providing teachers superior preparation prior to their careers and on-the-job support as they cope with the daily demands of their work. Rather than short-term solutions that aim to "fix" the problems of struggling students, many researchers and reformers favor systemic reform for sustained improvement. For example, the National Staff Development Council (NSDC), the premier think tank on professional development in the United States, has steadily revised its definition and norms for good professional development, leading a healthy dialogue on the right approach to work with schools (Box 2.1). They urge school systems to move away from the linear view critiqued by Fink and find solutions that go to the root of the problems that underlie low student achievement and engagement. The following excerpt is from the NSDC's recent policy statement issued in its position of partner to President Obama's administration in revising the education bill in the United States. It shows a clear move away from Input $\rightarrow$ Output–type thinking to an approach that is connected with the political, social, and cultural fabric of schools. Highlights of the amendments are excerpted below (National Staff Development Council, n.d.):

BOX 2.1

NSDC Proposed Amendments to Section 9101 (34) of the Elementary and Secondary Education Act

(34) PROFESSIONAL DEVELOPMENT—The term "professional development" means a comprehensive, sustained, and intensive approach to improving teachers' and principals' effectiveness in raising student achievement—

(A) Professional development fosters collective responsibility for improved student performance and must be comprised of professional learning that:

(1) is aligned with rigorous state student academic achievement standards as well as related local educational agency and school improvement goals;

(2) is conducted among educators at the school and facilitated by well-prepared school principals and/or school-based professional development coaches;

(3) primarily occurs several times per week among established teams of teachers, principals, and other instructional staff members where the teams of educators engage in a continuous cycle of improvement.

(B) The process outlined in (A) may be supported by activities such as courses, workshops, institutes, networks, and conferences that:

(1) must address the learning goals and objectives established for professional development by educators at the school level;

(Box 2.1 Continued)

(Box 2.1 Continued)

> (2)   advance the ongoing school-based professional development; and
> (3)   are provided by for-profit and nonprofit entities outside the school such as universities, education service agencies, technical assistance providers, networks of content-area specialists, and other education organizations and associations.

The limitations of a focused approach have forced educational researchers and practitioners to consider other alternatives. Slowly, a consensus supporting systemic reform developed, especially in the West, due to successful experiments in public school systems. Systemic reform approaches like whole school change, comprehensive school reform, and coalition-based efforts have spread since the 1980s. In the United States, for example, more than 300 "designs" for whole school reform have developed over the last few decades, many of which were grown in public systems, and still actively work with school districts across the country through long-term partnerships (Kilgore, 2006).

Systemic Partnerships

Michael Fullan (1990), the guru of whole school change and systemic approaches, writes:

> *Our attention in policy, practice, and research has shifted in recent years, away from preoccupation with single innovations toward more basic, integrative, and systematic reform. Changes in the culture of schools, in the roles and relationships of schools, districts, universities, and states, and in integrating teacher development, school improvement, leadership and curriculum toward more engaging learning experiences for students and teachers, dominate the current scene and will continue to do so for the rest of the decade. (p. 137)*

The following example of systemic reform in Puerto Rico illustrates the work of the Puerto Rico Math and Science Partnership (PR-MSP), which involves four universities within Puerto Rico, and the Puerto Rico Department of Education.

Gomez (2004) documents the first phase of this initiative, begun in 1993, which was funded by the National Science Foundation, and was a statewide partnership to improve science and mathematics education in Puerto Rico, the second largest education system in the United States (after New York City). He writes that previous efforts were "isolated" and did not really succeed in improving the system, which he describes as dysfunctional:

> *In 1993 when the reform was initiated, Puerto Rico's public edu-cation system ... was a highly centralized, dysfunctional system, serving over 650,000 students, 80% of whom come from families below the federally established poverty level, in 1,500 schools with 30,000 teachers. At the end of 10 years, the reform had effec-tively reached 800 schools, more than 50% of the system's schools. (p. 1)*

Gomez (2004) cites several areas of integrated effort including policy directives, school-based support, community involvement, formative and summative research, and student assessment. Specifically, the initia-tive involved:

- Involving the Governor, Department of Education, Superintendents, and the legislature to ensure that site-based management, accountability systems, and academic standards were uniform across the system.
- Supporting teachers, principals, and others within schools to become change agents in improvement efforts. Schools were identified as the units of change, and given significant auton-omy under the Community School law.
- Using a "Whole School Approach" that involved all Science and Math teachers and principals to acknowledge the need for improvement in these areas, and to take responsibility for the initiative in their school.
- Professional development of teachers through connecting them with the University partners, who prepared a teacher education curriculum, off-site in-services, and on-site coaching.
- In the scale-up period, schools showing high levels of improve-ment in each educational region were identified as Dissemination Centers and their capacity developed to act as resources to other schools in their region. Teachers from each center offered technical support in other schools for their respective regions.

- A system of assessment aligned with the reform used pre-tests and post-tests to look at student performance on varied types of assessments, including multiple choice, open-ended questions, and application of concepts.
- A focus on the school as the site of reform, enabling partners to work with schools directly and through Dissemination Centers.
- Ensuring that the community understood the initiative and supported it.
- Consolidating existing resources in the system so that they were used optimally.
- Studying the initiative to monitor implementation, as well as determine whether, and how much, the reform influences student achievement. (p. 5)

The website of the PR-MSP (Math and Science Partnership Network, n.d.) notes that currently,

...over 300 mathematics and science faculty and scientists from university partners and supporting organizations, forming four regional supporting teams, are working directly with K-12 Mathematics and science teachers and school and district personnel to provide professional development supporting the implementation and evaluation of challenging research-based curriculum and assessment to optimize math and science education for 305,000 students in 584 K-12 schools across the Island.

According to the site, the main activities of the PR-MSP include teacher preparation, professional development, in-school innovation, and action research. Specifically:

- The provision of new professional development and credentialing opportunities for mathematics and science teachers.
- Establishing Math and Science Resource Centers and a Math and Science Education Website to support improvement in all schools in Puerto Rico.
- Within schools, Learning Communities and Mathematics and Science Leading Teachers, work with partners on an ongoing basis.
- Teams of teachers, faculty, and researchers design field trips using the local context as science laboratory.

- Core partner universities are engaged in reform of teacher preparation programs reaching over 3,000 future K-12 teachers.
- Teams of teachers and faculty engage in action research to document teaching and learning in their classrooms.
- The impact of the PR-MSP on student achievement is measured through standardized tests based on TIMSS and NAEP assessments.

A recent report by the NSF (2010) states that the MSP was scaled up in 2002 to include the entire United States and Puerto Rico. The report lists the various policy/funding streams that have supported the project: Title II of the No Child Left Behind legislation; America Competes Act of 2007; and the American Recovery and Reinvestment Act of 2009. The U.S. Department of Education also coordinates its Math and Science programs with the NSF project.

The report states that longitudinal qualitative research conducted on the initiative shows that its implementation strategies of integrating teacher preparation, on-site coaching, curricular innovation, and connecting the local and national infrastructure through networking have helped the program connect deeply with schools, districts, universities, and state departments of education. The report also summarizes a national analysis of student outcomes between 2003 and 2007 on state assessments and found sustained gains in student achievement over the four-year period. The following is an excerpt from the report:

> *In mathematics, there was an overall increase in mathematics proficiency in MSP schools from the first year (2003–04; within 672 schools in the sample) to the end year (2006–07; within 1,666 schools in the sample) at all school levels. The sustained (first year to end year) increase in mathematics proficiency was found to be statistically significant at the elementary, middle, and high schools levels. Similar findings have been found for science at the elementary and middle school levels, as overall there have been strong increases for the entire MSP portfolio. (NSF, 2010, p. 10)*

Furthermore, the report emphasizes the closing of achievement gaps between African–American and Hispanic students with white students. Students with limited English proficiency also displayed gains, according to the report.

The MSP website provides actual percentage gains in test scores for a sample of 123 schools. It reports that (MSP, n.d.): "An analysis of 123 schools sampled for the study showed that students performance in Math improved by close to 14% in elementary, 6% in middle, and 17% in high school. In Science, the same groups improved by 5%, 4.5%, and 1% respectively."

While the Puerto Rico case shows us the complexity inherent in systemic reform, with its many layers of political, educational, and social concerns, it also shows how tying such reform to policy frameworks and funding streams can build a national movement for educational, specifically Math and Science, reform. Many now assert that systemic reform strategies tied to national, state, and local policies are an effective tool for long-term educational improvement (Aladjem & Borman, 2006). For example, in the 1990s, groups in Australia began pushing for American-style public school reform, driven by policy, and partnered by universities and educational organizations (Bosker, Creemers, & Stringfield, 1999). Several countries have independently arrived at the conclusion that systemic reform is needed to address problems in education such as the quality of teaching, student engagement and retention, and sustained and widespread improvement. Even the World Bank, long a supporter of cost-effective, scalable programs, has begun to consider systemic reform as the better alternative (WDR, 2004).

The Middle Start case in Chapter 3 illustrates a successful, long-term, multipronged approach to public education reform. While not country-wide like the Math and Science Partnership, Middle Start began as an experimental approach in a dozen schools in Michigan and steadily grew into a statewide effort. With funding from the federal budget for Comprehensive School Reform, Middle Start spread to other parts of the United States. Several other promising examples from developed and developing countries show that systemic reform has support from not just governments but also parents and educators. A recent report from the Organization for Economic Co-operation and Development (OECD, 2010) documents China's efforts at a more inclusive and decentralized education system with high levels of curricular rigor and strong teaching. Hopkins (2011) writes about systemic reform in Victoria, Australia, and its strong roots in long-term, large-scale, curricular, and pedagogical reform. Fullan (2009), in his recent publication on systemic reform, concludes that it has endured more than three decades of policy cycles and reform fads and has finally come into its own in places as diverse as Singapore and Finland. While not all of the above-mentioned cases of systemic reform were carried out through PPPs, the approach has been acknowledged as a powerful one by several government bodies over the past three decades.

However, even this system has detractors among those who support educational entrepreneurship as holding promise for the improvement of public systems. In a recent book, Hess and Manno (2011) disclaim whole school or comprehensive reform, saying it has not made a dent in the public education landscape and has instead created new bureaucracies that crush new entrants from bringing cutting-edge tools and technology into public schools. They push customization as the means to revitalize public systems. They argue for greater choice for parents and students in curricular and enrichment activities. They propose that "unbundling" the whole school reform package, and instead allowing the funds to be used for allowing varied providers to bring in curricular and co-curricular programs that correspond with parents' and students' needs and interests. Accessing the advantages of educational technology and virtual learning are important aspects of this approach. Hess and Manno stress that educating parents on the varied choices available to them is critical if they are to push for customized options that will boost school quality and student engagement.

There are at least three issues with customized schooling that need clarification. One, it is not clear if the approach sets limitations on entry for the kinds of providers or entrepreneurs who would be allowed to work with schools. In a coming section on motive, I discuss the case of Edison Schools and the choppy course of its engagement with the Philadelphia School District. Entrepreneurial approaches must be adequately scrutinized to see if they bring real benefits to schools and students. Two, it is not clear if there will be coordination of all the different approaches that could potentially work with a single school. If the customization occurs at the level of one parent or one student, there is truly a complex task of coordination involved for all students in the school to avail of their choices. A potential third issue is the likelihood of this becoming a new form of social stratification, as differential access to information on the parts of parents and students may cause some students being able to customize their schooling much better than others, and this may well pattern along already established lines of social class.

SCALE: EXPERIMENTAL/POLICY-DRIVEN

Experimental

The following case of environmental education in Thailand shows how a small project in one school grew to a pilot in seven schools, and went on to become a policy-driven model for the entire country within a few years. Going back to the discussion of partnerships, and why they are important in education reform—the needs of the lowest performing schools are immense and no single provider can do justice to resolving the issues that underlie low performance on their own. Education is a right in many countries, and unless we can promise reform of a certain quality and scale, we, as people interested in public education, cannot support the fulfillment of its lofty objectives. Scale is of great importance in public education, and though many of the best reform initiatives began as beautiful experiments serving a precious group, the goal of public school reform should be integration and scale-up of these experiments with policy directives and government financing to serve all students. SSA in India (Education for All) is a very pertinent example in this discussion of partnerships and education policy. It specifically invites educational organizations to partner with the government in large-scale reform of public education throughout the country. Unfortunately, independent research on the many efforts ongoing through SSA in India is sparse; it is difficult to judge the reach and quality of SSA partnerships. SSA is discussed in detail in the section on policy-driven efforts. The previous discussion of the Math and Science Partnership, its national reach and political support, also illustrates the significance of scale in public education reform efforts.

In the Thailand case, Andrew Bartlett and Marut Jatiket (2003) document the Rural Ecology and Agricultural Livelihoods (REAL) project's phenomenal growth from a one-school initiative to a country-wide network, which has influenced other countries in Asia to follow its example. According to the authors, REAL started in 1995 as a fifth grade project in a school in central Thailand when a teacher named Manas Burapa decided that his students needed field experience to fully understand the side effects of pesticides, and from this experience grasp the larger framework of rural ecology. Burapa involved the Agricultural Extension Department and an NGO called World Education (later Thai Education Foundation) in gathering all the information needed to run his fieldwork project.

Banharn Chantokomuth, a trainer from World Education, worked with Burapa on developing the curriculum for elementary students, and adapted material from the "Farmer Field School," a curriculum developed for adult farmers by the UN Food and Agriculture Organization (FAO). Kantamara, Hallinger, and Jatiket (2006) describe the students' activities in detail in their paper on the same program, which they refer to as the Integrated Pest Management (IPM) program:

Learning activities conducted by the students include field sur-
veys, extermination of insects, creation of insect zoos, data collec-
tion and analysis, problem-solving, and decision-making. These
occur in conjunction with the actual process of farming which
takes place throughout the planting season. In the IPM curricu-
lum, the learning process and context as well as the roles of stu-
dents and teachers contrast sharply with the passive learning that
characterizes the traditional Thai classroom.

The IPM program involves weekly sessions held in the field and
the classroom. First, students go into the field to discover through
direct experience every step of how to grow crops, either rice or
vegetables. During the season they are introduced to the stages of
the planting cycle: Pre-planting Stage, Seedling Stage, Vegetative
Stage, Productive Stage, Harvesting Stage, Post-harvesting Stage.
While in the field, they make detailed observations of the agro-
ecosystem. This involves identifying the names of insects, counting
their numbers and determining their location, observing whether
they are pests or natural enemies, measuring the level of water
and measuring the height of the plants.

Back in the classroom, the students document their fieldwork,
analyze and discuss the data they collected from observation.
These sessions, in the field and the classroom, are carried out by
students working in small groups. Every student becomes actively
involved in practical and analytical work. By exploring the actual
farming process that takes place in a rice field, students are intro-
duced to a wide range of environmental concepts and issues.
These include food chains and life cycles, water pollution and soil
erosion, and biodiversity. By learning through this active approach,
topics are transformed from a list of abstract concepts into a web
of tangible processes that matter to the students and their families.
Students become part of that web every time they enter a rice field,
and they learn how their own actions make a difference to other
parts of the web. (p. 10)

Simultaneously, the Ministry of Education was in the throes of
improving teaching methods in primary schools. According to Kantamara
et al. (2006), a comprehensive national educational reform law was
enacted in 1999 emphasizing literacy, numeracy, and IT capability,
alongside independent, life-long learning, student-centered approaches,
and decentralization. However, the rhetoric of the policy was difficult to
implement, given Thailand's deep-rooted traditions of rote learning and

top-down teaching. The Ministry was very interested in Burapa's approach of practical education with an environmental focus, as it was aligned with what they wanted to accomplish through policy changes. They decided to pilot the program in seven other schools. The program enjoyed a lot of press, and by 1998 Burapa was awarded a National Model Teacher award.

REAL introduced courses to support teachers as they conducted the practical and classroom components of the program. Parents became involved in providing study sites (their agricultural land) and participating in student surveys and discussions. Kantamara et al. (2006) write:

> *The curriculum involves parents and community members as knowledge resources for the students. They provide information on plant morphology, the planting calendar, and local pests. They assist on chemicals surveys and summarize inputs and profits. Community members become legitimate sources of indigenous knowledge that complements the formal scientific knowledge gained from classroom resources. (p. 10)*

The curriculum for farmers was adapted to provide students with a holistic perspective on agricultural practices, with a focus on their relationship with rural ecology. Students conducted field observations to understand activities within rice fields, which led them to many other topics. Bartlett and Jatiket (2003) write:

> *By exploring what is happening in a rice field, students can be introduced to a wide range of environmental issues such as food chains and life cycles, water pollution and soil erosion, biodiversity and genetic modification of crops. The information and materials which students collect in the field are used as a basis for science projects, math exercises, art activities, and essay writing assignments. Students are encouraged to keep portfolios of the work they produce, and exhibitions are organized to share this work with the community.*

Kantamara et al. (2006), who studied the program for its implications for educational policy, write that teachers had to significantly change their mindset and practices to use the curriculum:

> *The IPM curriculum is ... a radical change from the norm in Thai schools. It is no exaggeration to refer to IPM as a paradigm shift*

in learning method ... it also requires the development of new knowledge and skills among school personnel who undertake this program. Nonetheless, the presence of success stories throughout the country is itself a support factor. The schools in which the IPM curriculum is being used provide observable models of success. (p. 26)

The Ministry, the main sponsor of the program and its partners, Thai Education Foundation (TEF) and Manas Burapa, were strategic in their efforts to scale up REAL, so as not to dilute its quality. By the end of 2002, the program involved 48 schools in six provinces. The process employed for scaling up the program was exemplary: Each Thai province which had schools involved had its own professional development, planning, monitoring, and supervision structures. Kantamara et al. (2006) add, "Three of the provinces have also created their own 'eco-schools network' that helps teachers to exchange experience and materials." The FAO also funded part of the program, as a part of its IPM program. REAL has since been introduced in Bangladesh, Cambodia, Indonesia, Laos, and the Philippines. Government and nongovernment entities in these countries have taken the program to hundreds of schools.

Scaling up a program as nuanced as REAL included a multipronged approach, including:

- Recruiting new schools with the assurance that principals, teachers, parents, and community members supported what the new approach REAL stood for.
- Providing numerous teachers and principals the preparation and on-site support that implementing REAL required.
- Aligning curriculum, instruction, and assessment with the existing system in new schools.
- Integrating REAL with other subjects such as Math and Language within schools, which needed the interest and participation of teachers of these subjects.
- Condensing and timing teacher workshops so that teachers new to REAL could learn it during school breaks, and begin using it with on-site support during school terms.
- Developing a cadre of teacher trainers who provided on-site support in schools, as teachers piloted the REAL curriculum in new schools.

- Evaluating of the implementation and outcomes of the program in schools.
- Organizing networking meetings for schools for ongoing reinforcement and refinement.
- Raising funds to meet the needs of a rapid expansion, as there were sometimes delays in the funding from the ministry, due to bureaucratic procedures.
- Coping with changes in senior levels of the ministry, as each change brought variations in policy directives, and affected the expansion of REAL.

Kantamara et al. (2006) write about a paradoxical situation brought on when the Ministry decided to expand the program to every school in Thailand:

This was impossible given the human resources available. Unfortunately, this limitation then led decision-makers to withdraw broader financial support, which again left the implementers searching for funds. At this point, expansion of the IPM program continues to lack reliable central funding and must be cobbled together from a variety of sources. As a result, TEF was prompted to change the strategy towards building capacity of the Eco-Schools Network to develop proposals, solicit funding and manage their programs.

The aforementioned detailed case shows how close the Thai project came to receiving a mandate from the ministry, but was hobbled by its inability to keep up with the scale of teacher development and support that a nationwide implementation requires. Chapter 4 ends on this same note, as the Montessori project in Chennai's Corporation (public) schools also went through similar steps of expanding from one school to a city-wide effort, but ultimately remains challenged by the financial, human resource, and logistical constraints of going to scale.

These are very real concerns for reformers, as enhancing the quality of teaching and learning requires a nuanced and experimental approach, in most cases. Scaling up successful pilots needs partners to distance themselves from the school level to an extent, and focus their energies on setting up the institutions that will allow them to scale up the program instead. The case of Middle Start comprehensive school reform (CSR), in Chapter 3, describes in detail the growth of the program from a foundation-funded initiative to a federally funded and endorsed national design.

Policy-driven

Governments around the world, like the Thai Education Ministry, seem to be moving toward a larger view of education, stressing teacher quality and student engagement. Education policy in many countries has begun to look at promising regional pilots and give them the wherewithal to scale up. But the reality in many schools is that traditional methods of teaching and learning are still deep-rooted and take time to give way to other approaches. At present, approaches such as Montessori, Middle Start, and REAL coexist with those that have already rooted in the system, usually traditional rote and assessment-heavy approaches.

In Tamil Nadu, the Indian state in which I currently live, a policy directive from the Tamil Nadu State Department of Education through the vehicle of Sarva Shiksha Abhiyan (translated from Hindi it means "Education for All"), in partnership with the nonprofit Rishi Valley Education Center, part of the Krishnamurti Foundation India's (KFI) group of institutions, brought in activity-based learning (ABL) into the Corporation schools in Chennai, in 2003, starting from Class I. After successfully scaling up ABL in Chennai, the Ministry, in 2007, authorized its expansion into 10 schools per block[2] throughout the state of Tamil Nadu. The program continues till date, with support from the State government. A study conducted by S. Anandalakshmi (2007) provides a detailed documentation of the history of ABL and its implementation in Tamil Nadu. The ABL program has a specific set of curricular materials in the five subject areas of Tamil (language), English, Mathematics, Science, and Social Science. Anandalakshmi (2007) states:

In the ABL kit in Tamil Nadu, the subjects covered are five plus one. Tamil Language is the first area, where the lesson begins with illustrated cards and short words that are easy to write, rather than with the alphabet sequence. A similar method is used for teaching English. Mathematics is learnt through using the attractive Montessori materials, designed systematically, for the fundamental principles of addition, subtraction, multiplication and division. Science and Social Science cards are largely based on the textbook, with a variety of activities attached to every chapter. The sixth area is that of puppetry, story telling, reading of storybooks, paper craft, drawing, collage and many kinds of group games played outdoors. (p.7)

The physical structure of the ABL classroom keeps the child in mind, according to the researcher. The blackboard is at the child's eye level, and the size of the blackboard is increased to allow children space to work, and to show each other the work they simultaneously produce. Anandalakshmi writes:

By bringing the blackboard from the teacher's eye level to the child's, and by increasing the blackboard space, two more learning aids have been created: a specific space for each child to write and a large space to read each others' exercises. Every child can proudly own a part of that blackboard. (p. 7)

Self-evaluation through review using the assigned card at the end of each set of materials, allows the child to understand how much he or she has learned, and allows an opportunity for relearning what is still unclear. Anandalakshmi writes:

In building in the opportunity of recall of learnt material at each stage, evaluation has become part of the process. For the children, there is no failure and therefore, there is no fear of failure. In the conventional school system, so many children drop out of school because they fail! The need for an examination at the end of the school year is made redundant in this system. (p. 8)

Akila R. (2009) conducted a United Nations Children's Fund (UNICEF)-funded evaluation of ABL in Tamil Nadu from 2007 to 2008. Her detailed mixed-method, large-sample study covers 5 percent of the state's ABL schools, and includes over 3,000 classrooms. She provides a detailed description of the curricular materials, teachers' roles, learners' activities, and the system of learning and evaluation in her report. She describes multi-grade classrooms with children from Class 1 through 4 learning together. Children of different ability levels were folded into mixed ability groups. Each group represented a learning level, and a class typically had six groups. A single teacher worked with the group. The class size was usually around 40 children. Learning took place through small group discussions and activities, which were part of the "Learning ladder," the card-based curricular system of ABL. Akila (2009) describes the six groups in the following manner:

- *Group 1 and 2 are teacher supported, where every child learns the given concepts from the teacher on a one-to-one basis. The cards are so arranged in the sequence of milestones such that the zero milestone cards are completed within the first month of a child's admission. Basic competencies in each milestone are taught by the teacher to children in group 2 on a one-to-one basis. Practice of these competencies through activities continue in the other groups as children move to them.*
- *Group 3 is a partially teacher-support group. Children work with the relevant practice cards but seek teachers' help if needed. They also make use of the lower level blackboard in which space is allotted for every child. Later, this learning is reinforced by writing in their notebooks, which the teacher regularly checks.*
- *Group 4 presents reinforcement activities. This is a partially peer supported group. Being multi-grade, children in class 3 or 4 help those in lower grades to perform the activities mentioned in the cards. So, as the younger children learn something new, the older ones get a reinforcement of what they learnt earlier. In the process, any child may seek the help of teachers also.*
- *Group 5 is a fully peer-supported one, where children are comfortable to work in their own pace but along with the help of others in the group. Activities are of the enrichment kind for this group.*
- *Finally, as children gain mastery of each particular competency, they move to Group 6, a self-support group, where they test their learning through evaluation/test cards. The teacher marks the achievement of the child in the achievement chart displayed in the class, which the child also can check. This is basically a record of all children and their positions according to their completed milestones in the ladder. It is colour-coded for easy understanding. (p. 5)*

Akila (2009) writes that such self-initiated learning supports individual children's pace of learning. She also mentions the child eye-level blackboard that Anandalakshmi (2007) describes, saying that the blackboard has space allotted to each child. She describes the role of the blackboard thus:

Children are given a specific space to write and also a larger space to read others' works, as this is believed to reinforce learning. In fact, each activity is repeated three times by each child for reinforcement and mastery. First, upon reading from the card, they write in their notebooks, and then they move to their space in the blackboard, and finally write in their activity book. (p. 8)

Traditional forms of testing are replaced by self-evaluation cards that children complete after finishing a set of materials. If needed, they review and repeat the activities that they find challenging, in order to properly complete the self-evaluation, and more importantly, understand the material thoroughly. The teacher also maintains an evaluation chart to keep track of the pace and level of learning of every child. Akila emphasizes the productive nature of teacher–student interaction, and describes the teacher as a "guide" and a "friend" to students (Akila, 2009, p. 9).

Sarva Shiksha Abhiyan's ABL program in Tamil Nadu has won accolades within India and abroad for bringing about large-scale improvement in a state education system. Akila (2009) mentions some of the national recognition garnered the project:

Independent Joint Review Missions have acclaimed ABL as a holistic approach to enhance the quality of education at the primary level, the Ministry of Human Resource Development has commended it for its innovative quality improvement, and a Prime Ministers' award has been made in recognition of ABL's successful spread and reach.

A team from the World Bank and European Commission that visited ABL schools in Tamil Nadu in 2008 reports that students are energetic and fully engaged in learning activities. Teachers report that the system had helped them teach in an in-depth and interesting manner. The team summarizes their report with recommendations regarding additional support for children who advance at a slower pace, dividing the day into more slots, adding subjects and skills, enhancing the reading component, and integrating textbooks so children are familiar with their use as an additional resource. They write (World Bank, n.d.):

- *The ABL methodology provides an opportunity for children to proceed at their own pace of learning. However, accelerating progress of children lagging significantly behind their age appropriate class versus the progress along the learning ladder of children in their own age appropriate class may need to be monitored more closely and additional support provided.*

- *In terms of the daily schedule, there is merit in not binding the time table in 40 minutes slot as is the traditional practice. However, the ABL schedule of dividing the day into only two slots with forenoon dedicated to one curricular area and afternoon to another was observed to be very lengthy and tiring for small children. Given children's developmental status and needs at the primary stage, it would be desirable to have a better balance within each session of active versus passive and group versus individual activities. This may help to optimize children's participation, interest and learning.*

- *The curriculum at present focuses only on Language, Mathematics and EVS with a thrust on competencies. The team was happy to note that the state is considering making the curriculum more comprehensive to include art, crafts, music etc. In terms of Language curriculum also, it would be desirable to focus more on development of listening and speaking skills in children.*

- *It was very heartening for the team to observe children reading fairly fluently even from the newspapers or wall hoardings. These skills could be further enriched by providing children opportunities to "bond" with books and experience more meaningful and interesting reading through activities like story telling, story book selection and handling in book corners.*

- *Teachers appear to report some difficulties in effectively implementing ABL in large class sizes, whereas it works very well for small class sizes. Teachers appear to have some difficulty in addressing a classroom that has large numbers of class 3 and 4 children who demand and occupy greater attention of the teachers than the class 1 and 2 children. (Possibility to group children in different ways was also raised and the SSA management has given the freedom to the teacher to organize her class in the way she considers most appropriate.)*

- *The ABL has completely dispensed with the textbooks in the classrooms—although the State continues to provide textbooks to all children, they are kept outside of classrooms, to be consulted only once in a while. It would be advisable to see these text books as additional resource materials to be used in more creative and imaginative ways rather than keep them*

out of the classrooms, which may adversely condition children
towards books. (p. 6)

Despite these areas for growth, ABL represents a clear shift away from the traditional classrooms that were typical of government schools in Chennai and the rest of Tamil Nadu. A 2010 report on the main activities under SSA in Tamil Nadu by SSA states that ABL has brought about "a metamorphosis" in the quality of teaching in schools, and confidence and enthusiasm for learning among students. The following is an excerpt from the website (Sarva Shiksha Abhiyan, 2010):

The new methodologies with the support of fully trained teachers
effectively address the maladies which the traditional system of
teaching–learning has been suffering from. There has been visible
changes and complete transformation in the classroom processes
with the children actively participating in their own learning and
the teachers playing the role of facilitators. The classroom pro-
cesses have undergone a metamorphosis with children exhibiting
unlimited curiosity, interest and enthusiasm for learning. The
classroom space has been transformed in to a comfortable zone
for the children. It has also been observed that the confidence
levels of children have greatly improved. (p. 1)

According to newspaper reports, ABL in Tamil Nadu government schools has attracted the attention of educational authorities in other developing countries. Delegations from Bangladesh and China visited Tamil Nadu schools last year to study ABL at work, and to see if it would fit their public systems. The *Hindu* reports (2009):

At the end of a visit to some of the government primary schools in
the southern suburbs of Chennai, a 12-member delegation of offi-
cials of the Ministry of Primary and Mass Education from the
government of Bangladesh, said Tamil Nadu's model of primary
education was apt to be followed in their country which was fac-
ing low literacy levels and a high dropout rate in the primary
section.

A similar delegation comprising education department officials and school teachers from China went a step further and sought the help of the Tamil Nadu government in launching ABL in China on an experimental basis, according to another newspaper article by Mallady (2009):

*A communication was received from officials in China following
a recent visit of a Chinese delegation that undertook a study tour
to various schools in which ABL is implemented under the Sarva
Shiksha Abhiyan programme and saw for themselves the classroom practices. M.P. Vijayakumar, Honorary Advisor, SSA
(Tamil Nadu), told The Hindu here on Sunday that resource support was sought from Tamil Nadu for launching the innovative
teaching–learning methodology in China on an experimental
basis.*

Interestingly, there is some debate about what the ABL/SSA partnership has meant for student achievement, measured in hard numbers,
in Tamil Nadu. An article by Raghupathi (2009) reports that test data
from the National Center for Education Research and Testing (NCERT),
a national body, and literacy and numeracy data gathered by the independent NGO Pratham, as part of their large scale annual survey for a
similar period in a similar age group, present significantly different
pictures of student learning in Tamil Nadu. Raghupathi shows that the
Tamil Nadu's 34,342 primary schools with an aggregate enrolment of
6.2 million children,

*... rank 20 percent below the national average in reading and
mathematical abilities of students. The ASER survey further indicates that only 54.7 percent of children in classes I–II in this state
can read the alphabet against the national average of 75.4 percent. Similarly, of the children in classes II–V, only 45.7 percent
can read a simple (Tamil) language text, against the national
average of 66.6 percent. In terms of mathematical ability, only
62.6 percent of the children in classes I and II can identify numbers against the national average of 75.7 percent; and a mere 36.3
percent in classes III–V can do subtraction (54.9 percent).*

Raghupathi notes that the findings of ASER 2008 (Pratham, n.d.)
in Tamil Nadu contradict the national Midterm Assessment Survey or
MAS of class III children (SSA, n.d). This survey was "according to
the NCERT survey, Tamil Nadu's primary school children rank first in
maths ability and language skills with an average of 75.2 percent and
79.74 percent respectively." I could find no convincing explanations
for the discrepancy, but two evaluations by Schoolscape (2009) and
Akila R. (2009) both report significant gains in student achievement,

and the reduction of achievement gaps across socioeconomic and gender groupings.

Schoolscape, an educational organization commissioned by SSA, Tamil Nadu, to conduct an independent evaluation of ABL, carried out a one-year study in comprising of a baseline and follow-up assessment in the academic year 2007–08. The assessments were administered to students in Class II and IV in 750 schools spanning 30 districts in the subjects Tamil, English, and Mathematics, the baseline in June 2007, and the follow-up in April 2008. A reading test was also administered in Tamil and English in addition to written tests. Schoolscape's study showed significant gains in all subjects between the baseline and end of year tests, reduced gaps between gender and socioeconomic groups, and higher achievement bands for all groups in comparison to the baseline. Schoolscape's (2009) key findings are as follows:

- **Average achievement of children increased significantly in all subjects:** During the end-year study the average achievement was found to be 61.63 percent in Tamil, 74.45 percent in Mathematics, and 70.62 percent in English in Class II; and in Class IV, the mean achievement in Tamil was 63.19, 63.01 percent in Mathematics, and in English it was 52.33 percent. The figures revealed that as compared to the baseline study there was an increase of nearly 25 percent to 29 percent in all three subjects in both the classes. Maximum improvement was found in Thanjavur and minimum improvement was found in Chennai.
- **Gaps in achievement within gender, location and social groups were narrowed down:** During baseline study, there was significant difference in achievement between boys and girls, urban and rural children, and children from different social communities. However, during the end-of-the-year study, it was found that no significant difference was found in Tamil achievement between rural and urban children and among the children of different social groups; in Mathematics achievement, there was significant difference found between boys and girls and children of different social group children; in English achievement, there was no significant difference between rural and urban and among boys and girls.
- **More children shifted from low achievement range to very high and excellent achievement range:** Number of low achievers reduced by 30–40 percent in all three subjects in both

the classes and number of excellent achievers increased by 20–40 percent in all three subjects and both classes.

- **Dispersion in children's achievement was reduced:** The standard deviation in achievement score in all subjects and most of the groups was reduced; it revealed a homogeneous performance in learning achievement during the 2008 test as compared to 2007. (p. 1)

The second evaluation was conducted by Akila R. (2009), also commissioned by SSA, and funded by UNICEF. This evaluation included students in classes 1–4 in 1,832 schools across Tamil Nadu in the 2008–09 academic year. The school represented 5 percent of the state's government and government-aided schools, including schools in educationally backward blocks. The study included 3,122 ABL classrooms and assessed the level and quality of implementation of ABL, as well as assessed student progress in Tamil, English, and Mathematics.

Akila writes that higher levels of ABL implementation indicated by the correct teaching methods, rich use of the materials and blackboards, regular self-evaluation by students, and monitoring by the teacher is highly correlated with students' performance on Ladder 3 tests. She reports on test results from tests at the mid-course of the ABL ladder—Ladder 3—in which over 20,000 students participated, finding that ABL has helped students boost achievement, reduce gaps between socioeconomic groups, and overcome disadvantages of low parental educational levels and incomes. These data corroborate the study by Schoolscape, cited earlier, which found similar patterns of achievement, and reduction of achievement gaps.

Akila concludes her report by terming ABL a trigger for social change, with the potential to make government schools as good as, or better than, aided schools. She writes (2009):

As [a] system intervention, ABL's positive impact has been well identified in this Evaluation. In all the core chapters of analysis, enough evidence has pointed that children learn just as well in the government schools as they do in the aided schools (which children of better socio-economic classes attend), because of the way the children are facilitated to learn. There have been hardly any differences in learning based on sex or community. This is a positive breakthrough indicating equitable learning levels among vast numbers of children, thus making the differential poverty levels,

parental educational status, etc. as negligible factors, once good
learning systems are in place. In this context, ABL can be seen as
a social change agent, as poorer and disadvantaged children also
gain equitable learning skills, and may thus be better equipped to
use other developmental opportunity later in life, which bud from
the functional literacy status. Thus, it has functioned as a learning
trigger, with wide-spread impact on quantity-quality improvement
in primary education. (p. 147)

Building in research and evaluation has served SSA–ABL we l, as
both Schoolscape and Akila R. indicate that there are variations in
implementation, and the World Bank team identifies several areas for
improvement, which in turn can inform future directions for the initiative. The almost decade-old initiative continues to move in a strong
direction in Tamil Nadu and remains a sterling example of a working
partnership between the government and a reputed nonprofit organization to bring about statewide reforms with policy backing. The Active
Learning Methodology (ALM) initiative for the middle and high school
also began in 2008 within the Chennai Corporation. Designed on similar
lines to the primary school initiative, ALM is conducted by SSA in partnership with the Krishnamurti Foundation India's (KFI) Chennai-based
school, The School, which has made available its system of curriculum
and instruction, along with teacher professional development and on-site
support to the Corporation (Sarva Shiksha Abhiyan and Krishnamurti of
India, 2008). Unlike the Thai case, the reforms continue and are even
permeating the K-12 spectrum, showing that large-scale, policy-driven
partnerships can be a "trigger" for significant education improvement.

TAKEOVER/COMPLEMENTARY

Takeover

The takeover, heralded as a tool of systemic reform by some, is very
controversial. The reader cannot miss the irony of listing this approach
in a discussion of different kinds of "partnerships." However, it is relevant to this discussion, as it is seen as a last resort measure (by some) in
places where public education dismally fails to do its job. Travers (2003)
documents the early years of the Philadelphia takeover, which was front-
page news for some weeks in the United States in 2001. She cites the

New York Times, which stated: "The state has taken over the school system, which had been failing for years and brought in seven outside managers to run 45 of the lowest performing elementary and middle schools." Travers carefully documents a school district with a complicated and inequitable pattern of state financing, very low student achievement despite several attempts at reform, and an ideological stance favoring private management in public schools, as she shows how the takeover occurred, and what its implications were over the ensuing period.

To summarize Travers' (2003) detailed discussion of the main steps of the takeover:

- The district hired Edison, Inc., a for-profit educational management company, to study the conditions in the district and propose a plan for the takeover. Edison, in its report proposed that the 100 lowest performing schools should be managed by private entities and that the Board of Education should be replaced with a School Reform Commission (SRC), headed by a CEO.
- This plan was approved by the city and state, setting the stage for a "friendly takeover." The state began the process of forming an SRC, which would run the district and hire the CEO. While the state and district had relatively smooth negotiations, students, community members and others actively protested the composition of the SRC, leading to changes in its composition. The state appointed a chair for the SRC, who was prompt in contracting Edison to manage 60 of the lowest performing schools.
- Several groups contested the process of hiring Edison, which pushed the SRC to open up the process and follow a "diverse provider" model, including for-profit and nonprofit organizations. According to Travers:

The final list of providers included three private, for-profit companies (Edison, Victory, and Chancellor Beacon), two private, not-for-profit companies (Foundations and Universal), and two universities (the University of Pennsylvania and Temple University); each of these were identified for "partnerships" with schools in the district. Edison was paired with 20 schools. Other providers, including the universities, were assigned between 3 and 5 schools each.

A total of 86 elementary and middle schools were divided up among providers. Travers notes that controversies raged over school selection, outsourcing of district services such as food and transportation, among other issues.

- The diverse provider model allowed for differences in the approach that each provider would follow in their set of schools. According to Travers: "The approaches varied in terms of their underlying philosophy and the types of curriculum and instruction they proposed."
- Travers, interestingly, notes that there was an element of competition among the providers, on the part of the public, and the SRC. She writes: "The public and the SRC perceived the various approaches as competing with each other to see which would succeed in improving the low-performing schools, and especially student test scores in those schools." This dramatic scenario became even more charged when Paul Vallas from the School District of Chicago was hired as the CEO in 2002, as Vallas had strong supporters and detractors among the school reform community. He kept some of the initiatives of the SRC and added his own, including a strict disciplinary policy, elimination of middle schools and reinstatement of K-8 schools, smaller high schools, and extended day and summer school for students failing on standardized tests.

Travers' account of the takeover is very detailed and intriguing, and those interested in the intricacies of this story must read her text. Takeovers made news in the United States in the 1990s, and have continued to make news in large American cities through the 2000s. Los Angeles faced a takeover in 2007 (Ramirez, 2007), and Milwaukee and Kansas City witnessed heated and long drawn-out battles for and against a takeover even more recently.

The jury is still out on whether mayoral reform has any role to play in improving teaching and learning and boosting student achievement in public systems within large cities. The small but well-researched body of work on their implications and long-term impact indicates that there is no clear proof that mayoral reform is linked to gains in student achievement and qualitative improvements to curriculum, instruction, or student engagement (Henig & Rich, 2004). The editors of the Harvard Educational Review compiled an analysis of takeovers, in which senior

educational scholars pondered the issue of whether or not this phenomenon was beneficial for public schools. The editors of the issue clearly
state that after reviewing several cases of mayoral takeovers they conclude that takeovers have not succeeded in bringing about significant
improvement in public schools and systems. They write (*Harvard
Education Review*, 2006):

> *Our authors agree that most mayoral involvement in education—
> including takeovers—is grounded in the mayors' genuine desire to
> make their schools better. And while our authors also agree that
> the impact of this involvement is usually more salutary than detri-
> mental, they offer some cautions as well. ... With fifteen years of
> history to draw on, some conclusions now can be made about
> whether this takeover movement has fully lived up to the optimistic
> predictions of its proponents. ... In our view, the answer is clear:
> It has not. ... Finally, we hope the mayor will recognize that
> although a school district takeover may produce a policy environ-
> ment that is conducive to dramatic reform, there is a difference
> between quick reform and meaningful reform. Mayoral takeovers
> of school districts may be a way to get things done—but the chal-
> lenge is to figure out the right things to do.*

Simmons, Foley, and Ucelli (2006) point out that takeovers, like
many other reform approaches, are merely a vehicle or format for reform
and it is the intent and content of the reform that has implications for
student learning. They state that often takeovers are about management
and streamlining systems and do not get to the heart of changing teaching and learning at the school level. Like the other authors cited earlier,
they agree that the direst situations may require a takeover, but caution
that this approach may worsen the situation, unless there is a strong
focus on teaching and learning.

Wong and Shen (2003) discuss the effect of takeovers on student
achievement, management, and accountability through a meta-study of
14 school US school districts. They point out that the No Child Left
Behind Act of 2001 institutionalizes takeovers as a strategy allowed in
the lowest performing districts. They state that there are few studies
that look across districts that have been taken over, and attempt to fill
this gap with their research on 14 major takeovers. They present a
comprehensive set of findings on takeovers, of which I highlight the
following:

- Mayoral takeovers are correlated with increases in student achievement at the elementary grades, but not in the upper grades.
- Student achievement suffers if there is political turmoil during and after a takeover.
- The biggest gains are in the lowest performing schools, owing possibly to increased attention to this subset of schools (p. 4).

My searches for literature on takeovers or similar methods in other countries yielded almost no results of citywide or larger-scale takeovers. Takeovers seem to be an American approach to bringing managerial expertise to large systems. However, it appears that managerial expertise alone will not bring about the classroom- and school-level changes that characterize the type of reform that MSP, REAL or ABL were able to bring about. The experience, expertise, and commitment to public education that these private entities brought to their work are missing from this administrative approach to reform.

Complementary

The term "complementary" partnership does not have a literature base, unlike the other types reviewed so far. This is probably because the assumption is that partnerships are collaborative and complementary, and neither partner intends to take over or undermine the other as they conduct their joint venture. However, in the context of takeovers, which are neither collaborative nor complementary, I want to briefly dwell on complementary partnerships and note that they are the "assumed" mode of code of conduct in most cases. Pratham and remedial education, the Math Science Partnership in Puerto Rico, REAL in Thailand, ABL in Tamil Nadu, and the two cases that form the core of this book, are all good examples of complementary partnerships, where public and private entities work together in a collaborative manner to bring about needed changes to teaching and learning. Therefore, a complementary partnership can be remedial or systemic in scope; and scale-wise, it can be experimental or policy-driven.

A complementary partnership may arise from a memorandum of understanding, an informal understanding, or a clear policy directive, as we can cull from the cases discussed in previous sections. Public and private partners may not have clear-cut roles to begin with, but it is clear from the beginning that there is no "takeover" of responsibility, and the private partner is not filling deficits or gaps in the existing system, but are instead adding value to what exists. Several of the examples in this book show that public partners have invited private entities to work in the system as part of a policy directive, as in the case of ABL, or have welcomed their initiative to conduct a pilot, as in the case of REAL. There was limited, or no, opposition to their work in public schools. This was unlike the takeover in Philadelphia and the animosity with which the schools, community, and observers reacted when told that the district was being handed over to a CEO, and that a for-profit company, Edison Schools, was to manage the majority of the schools in the district.

As Simmons et al. have said, dire circumstances may require a takeover, and it is difficult to say whether takeovers as a genre are to be avoided. However, in the cases where it is possible to conduct the work in a spirit of partnership, it is safe to say that the work is likely to proceed with less opposition and controversy, and allow for the benefits of collaborative discussion, problem solving, and a smoother implementation.

PROFIT/SOCIAL

Profit vs. social is a heated debate in education, as one country after the other opens its public schools to partnerships with external organizations. All of the cases discussed earlier, except the takeover involving Edison Schools, profiled nonprofit entities in partnership with governments and it was clear that there was no financial gain accruing to private partners through their participation in a PPP. For-profit companies that gain entry into public schools blur these lines, as they take control of school finances, and seek to bring in efficiencies that will generate profits for their companies. Like takeovers, for-profits are less likely to be "partners" to the government, and more likely to be contractors. Market-based approaches have been extensively studied in the United States, as they are of interest to politically conservative and liberal scholars, and have spawned variants such as charter schools, voucher programs, and Educational Management Organizations (EMOs) running public schools. Chile, Sweden, and Hong Kong have significant voucher programs, and private management of public schools is part of newer educational legislation in India as well.

The ideas of the American economist and Nobel laureate Milton Friedman are widely cited as the origin of the privatization movement in education. Friedman (1955, 1962) emphasized that the monopolistic nature of public systems: (*a*) denies parents free choice in their children's education, and (*b*) reduces the efficiency of the system over time. Ball and Youdell (2007) briefly outline the history of privatization stating that the US and then the UK experimented with different forms of privatization in education in the 1980s, and both countries revived these initiatives in the 2000s. They cite Chile and New Zealand as other countries that were early adopters of privatization of education on a large scale through policy-backed initiatives. They write about two forms of privatization—privatization "in" and privatization "of" public education:

- *Privatisation in Public Education or "endogenous" privatisation*
  These forms of privatisation involve the importing of ideas, techniques and practices from the private sector in order to make the public sector more like businesses and more business-like.
- *Privatisation of Public Education or "exogenous" privatisation*
  These forms or privatisation involve the opening up of public education services to private sector participation on a for-profit basis and using the private sector to design, manage or deliver aspects of public education. (p. 13)

Chubb and Moe (1990) have argued that privatization of education can achieve better outcomes at a lower cost, as well as force ailing public systems to improve themselves due to the fear of losing students. They also state that the private schooling can boost student achievement at a lower level of spending per pupil. Private involvement in the United States and in other countries often takes the form of charter or privately managed public schools. School voucher programs, often referred to in the same breath as charters, are quite different, as they provide a subsidy for public school parents to send their child to a private school. I do not discuss them in this section, as this approach is not about reforming public education through any form of partnership or public–private interaction, and instead enables public school students to attend private schools.[3]

Toch (1999) discusses the market-based movement in education in the United States in the 1990s and the math that made public schools attractive to private companies in that era when the educational entrepreneurship struck deep roots. He cites the example of Edison Schools (renamed Edison Learning), which became one of the largest companies to work with public systems. He writes:

> *Edison's successful IPO [initial public offering] reflects the momentum behind a market-based movement that is changing the very nature of public education. ... Edison is merely the largest of many new providers of public education that are now vying with traditional public schools for students. Churches, YMCAs, universities, at least two dozen for-profit companies and many other types of organizations are operating publicly funded charter schools and, in Edison's case, traditional public schools under contract to local school boards. ... The company is counting on such things as cheaper computers and economies of scale to put the company into the black. If the company grew to about 700 schools, it would have the revenues of a Fortune 500 company.*

EMO has become a blanket term that describes charter schools and privately managed public schools. Garcia, Barber, and Molnar (2009) review the literature on EMOs, summarizing them as follows:

> *...for-profit companies that provide "whole-school operation" services to schools. ... Although public schools have outsourced or contracted with private providers for some time, EMOs are distinct because they have executive authority over the operation and management of schools... including decisions about curriculum and instruction. In recent years, EMOs have proliferated in large part because of the increase in the number of charter schools.*

But do for-profit approaches count as public interest partnerships? Several articles on for-profits running charter schools and managing public schools mention the following pros and cons: Yes, students get a cleaner, safer school when it is managed by a for-profit organization (Henschtke, Oschman, & Snell, 2002), but the teachers tend to be less qualified as they can then be paid less, and the curriculum is more structured so that it is easier to teach (Molnar & Garcia, 2007). In many previous examples, where nonprofits undertook partnerships with the government, the heart of their efforts lay in strengthening teaching through workshops, on-site support, and materials. The focus was on learning that was engaging to students and integration of school learning with real-life experiences. In the Thai case, it was notable that the nonprofit institution lost government support because of its inability to scale up statewide at the pace the government required, because of its nuanced curricular and instructional approaches. ABL has been scaling up for the past 7 years in Tamil Nadu, and has to balance the state's need to universalize this approach with implementing its intricate curricular and instructional framework with integrity. The intent in these cases is not to get the per-pupil cost in hand or scale up and reap efficiencies to turn a profit, or like Edison, become a company whose performance drives its stock value.

Hentschke et al. (2002) list the following advantages for EMO-managed schools:

- Streamlined operations due to EMO's managerial expertise.
- Cleaner, safer schools for less-privileged children, which resemble good private schools in their infrastructure.
- Less absenteeism and dropout, as seen in some studies of EMO-run schools.
- Focus on improving basic skills such as reading and math, using packaged programs with a proven track record.
- Increases in test scores in comparisons with non-EMO public schools.

Garcia et al. (2009) identify the following concerns with EMO involvement in public schools:

- Cost-cutting measures that may sacrifice educational quality.
- Lack of diversity in curricular and instructional approaches. Use of packaged, direct instruction instructional approaches.
- Prevalence of rote learning and test-oriented learning.
- Less-qualified, less-experienced teachers.
- Lack of attention to differently-abled students
- Good test results on basic skills; poor results on tests of higher order thinking skills, when compared to like public schools.

Predictably, there is controversy on the topic of whether EMO-managed schools have improved student achievement on standardized measures, as proponents and opponents have each been able to produce assessments that support their stance.

Again, predictably, EMOs have produced study after study that shows significant gains in student achievement, using comparisons with non-EMO public schools. Proponents of charter reform, such as Caroline Hoxby, claim there are significant increases in comparison studies, and that the increases are proportional to the number of years charters have been in existence, as well as the public funding going into the charter. Hoxby (2004)[4] conducted a study of "the achievement of 99% of fourth graders who attend charter schools," and found that:

> *Students in charter schools that have been in operation longer are more likely to have a proficiency advantage over their peers in the matched regular public school. In reading, the advantage is 2.5 percent for a charter school that has been operating 1 to 4 years, 5.2 percent for a school operating 5 to 8 years, and 10.1 percent for a school operating 9 to 11 years. Also, charter school students are more likely to have a proficiency advantage if their school has funding that is at least forty percent of that enjoyed by regular public schools. The results suggest that charter schools are especially likely to raise the achievement of students who are poor or Hispanic. (p.3)*

Hoxby, Murarka, and Kang (2009) report huge gains for charter school students in a recent evaluation of New York City charter schools, which used random assignment through a lottery and public school comparisons. They found that charter schools in New York City cater to more minorities and low income students, and that these students showed great gains over the period of the study and closed achievement gaps as compared to students in traditional public schools. The term Scarsdale–Harlem contrasts the wealthy suburb or Scarsdale, NY, with Harlem, an inner-city lower-income neighborhood. The Scarsdale–Harlem achievement gap refers to the differences in student achievement in these two neighborhoods. They write:

> *On average, a student who attended a charter school for all of grades kindergarten through eight would close about 86 percent of the "Scarsdale-Harlem achievement gap" in math and 66 percent of the achievement gap in English. A student who attended fewer grades would improve by a commensurately smaller amount. ...On average, a lotteried-out student who stayed in the traditional public schools for all of grades kindergarten through eight would stay on grade level but would not close the "Scarsdale-Harlem achievement gap" by much.*

The numbers mentioned have been challenged by a number of researchers. DiCarlo (2011) raises methodological issues as well as critiques the method of calculating the gains in math and English. He also points out an error of omission: Science and Social studies scores have not been reported, as they did not record significant gains. A review of the literature on charter schools in comparison to public schools by Blazer (2010) also notes various critiques of Hoxby (2004), and Hoxby et al. (2009) including statistical errors, and overstatement of results.

Other researchers find great variation in student achievment in charter schools. The Center for Research on Education Outcomes (CREDO) at Stanford University conducted a longitudinal study of more than 70 percent of the students in charter schools in the United States, covering several states. In this national study, CREDO (2009) found:

Of charter schools, 17 percent provide superior education opportunities for their students. Nearly half of the charter schools nationwide have results that are no different from the local public school options and over a third, 37 percent, deliver learning results that are significantly worse than their students would have realized had they remained in traditional public schools.

The National Alliance for Public Charter Schools (2010), a proponent of this approach, conducted a meta-analysis of 203 studies on the impact of charter schools on student achievement. The criteria for inclusion of these studies are (*a*) charter school achievement is compared with that of traditional public schools, (*b*) the studies use rigorous methods, and (*c*) they have a significant sample size. This report looks at this large pool of data from several angles, and notes that the studies that report significant gains for students in charter schools are on the rise, compared to previous years; newer studies examining charters are showing gains in student achievement in comparison to public schools; and students who stay in charters for longer periods show greater gains over time.

An interesting study of charter school achievement by Garcia et al. (2009), which looked at students' learning in terms of their grasp of basic skills and higher order thinking skills, found that EMO–managed charter schools seemed to focus more on "skilling" children with basic, rather than higher order thinking skills. They write: "For students who remained in the same sector and same school for 3 consecutive years, EMO-managed charter schools exhibited a positive effect in reading vocabulary, a basic skills subtest, and a negative effect in reading comprehension, the complex thinking subtest." The authors conclude that this implies that the heavy focus on drill and practice in such schools are usually delivered by less qualified teachers, and this may be associated with a better grasp of basic mathematics and language, but gaps in overall comprehension of concepts and capacity for complex thought. They conclude:

> As profit-seeking enterprises, EMOs respond to the incentives provided by the legal and financial systems in which they operate. The bottom line is that for-profit schools must spend less than they collect. In so doing, EMO-managed charter schools face an internal conflict between cost savings and quality of education.

This section concludes without a clear direction for arguments pro and against charters, as there is not yet conclusive evidence around EMO-managed schools. The research is clouded, as it appears that arguments pro and con are being offered by groups with ideological positions, rather than by independent researchers who can interpret such schools with an open mind.

So, dear reader, where are we with all this? I've spilt much ink analyzing the different types of partnerships, and it seems that several governments are throwing in their support for PPPs with private entities and that much of what happens to students and their education rests with such entities. The experiment in Thailand, the partnership for Math and Science in Puerto Rico, and ABL in Tamil Nadu, India, are evidence of a positive trend in public education, where the fundamentals of teaching and learning have been touched and improved. Sustainability is the lasting question in many PPP initiatives, but where the social goal is up front and center there is no murky subtext underlying the intent, quality, and scalability of the initiative. However, there are clearly issues that need to be resolved before we declare it safe for governments to allow for-profits to manage public schools through methods such as takeovers, as otherwise we face a paradox, a blurring of lines between private and public leading to contradictions in the intent and content of public education.

This chapter reviewed four types of partnerships according to scope (focused or systemic); scale (experimental or policy-driven); method (takeover or complementary); and motive (profit or social). In each case, the discussion focused on whether or not the type of partnership improved student engagement and learning, through focusing on improved teaching. The scale at which the partnership functioned and its sustainability were also highlighted, and reasons for projects scaling and sustaining and for them not accomplishing these objectives were brought out. It was clear from the cases discussed that there is no clear answer on what ultimately satisfies all the criteria—of quality, scale, and sustainability. Also, it was clear that it is not at all clear whether any of the types can consistently satisfy the stringent requirements important to governments, the public, and funding organizations, of whether or not they raise student achievement on standardized tests.

Thus, the chapter may have raised more issues than it solved. After many years of engagement in education reform, I am satisfied with that result, as the only clear principles emerging from reforms all over the world are as follows:

1. Real school and classroom-level change are difficult.
2. The heart of reform should be improving teaching to improve learning.
3. Reform is a long-term process and is sensitive to the context, players, approach, funding, and many other factors.
4. Reform must be embedded in a system in order to scale up with integrity to its core principles, and sustain in the long term.

So, after many months of reading the literature on partnerships, sorting through it, creating the four types, and figuring out if they add value or not, my stand is that partnerships are a real asset in reform, and whether or not policy and student achievement targets are met, they offer more stability, quality, and support than other methods that have been tried. Of the types discussed, I would support systemic reform in partnership with experienced, reputed, nonprofits, clear about the kinds of teaching and learning they want to see in schools, and committed to improving public education.

We now move on to two cases of systemic reform, one in the United States and the other in India, as different as these two countries are but similar in their findings that partnerships can be forged between private and public entities, and steadily infuse systems with good teaching and learning. The cases also demonstrate the challenges involved in accomplishing the criteria of scale and sustaining the initiative through policy cycles and other changes that occur in the normal course of an initiative.

NOTES

1. Consider the use of the word "treatment" and "control" in randomized evaluations in education.
2. A block is an administrative unit. Several blocks make up a district. There are 32 districts in the state of Tamil Nadu. Each district has 10–20 blocks, depending on the size of the district and its urban–rural composition.
3. For arguments against school vouchers, see Kohn and Shannon (2002). Also see Rouse and Barrow (2008) for a meta-analysis of evidence supporting school vouchers.
4. Hoxby's work has been challenged by Rothstein (2004), who shows that the claims are overstated

3

Middle Start in American Public Schools

This chapter describes the first case that makes up the core of this book on educational partnerships, and is based on 10 years in the life of Middle Start, an initiative to bring about improvement in the middle grades in American public schools. Middle Start began in 1994 in Michigan as a pilot effort to improve 12 schools in rural and urban areas of Michigan that were low performing.[1] Sponsored by the W.K. Kellogg Foundation (WKKF) in Battle Creek, Michigan, and designed and implemented by the Academy for Educational Development (AED),[2] an educational nonprofit organization based in New York, the effort evolved over the next 10 years into a large-scale partnership called the Michigan Middle Start Partnership (MMSP) headed by WKKF and AED, and included schools, school districts, the State Department of Education, and several regional educational organizations (such as universities). The development of this partnership was partially strategic and partially organic, as the initiative began to seek partners to improve its conceptual clarity and quality of implementation, as well as root itself in existing structures in the state to ensure scale and sustainability of middle-grades reform.

Middle Start's evolution and ongoing refinement marched alongside dramatic support on the part of the federal government for comprehensive school reform (CSR) in the No Child Left Behind (NCLB) legislation. CSR became a widely accepted method of working with schools, and in the late 1990s and before 2005 several of the neediest, lowest-performing schools received grants from Departments of Education in different states to work with proven models of school improvement, of which Middle Start was one. Thus, this chapter, alongside the story of the Middle Start, also discusses the roles of the federal, state, and district authorities in collaborating with CSR models through providing access to schools, conducting reviews of the quality of models, initiating longitudinal research and evaluation, and connecting schools and models with regional educational agencies (called "laboratories") that provided varied services and resources to models and schools. The CSR section of the NCLB Act also granted each school up to US$50,000 per year to work with a model, with the option to renew the grant each year for 3 years.

This chapter is a case study of the layers within which a school is embedded, and how any process of change and improvement must embrace all the layers. The success of Middle Start depended on the coordination and cooperation of several stakeholders, and their united, and multipronged efforts to build on the strengths of schools and systems. Drawing on several longitudinal qualitative and quantitative studies, I piece together the story of this successful partnership at the school, school district, and organizational levels in Michigan, outlining its history, implementation process, and academic and other outcomes. In this effort, I draw on my own research on Middle Start, published work by my former colleagues within AED, as well as summative evaluations by third-party evaluators of Middle Start.[3]

Writing this chapter has been a bittersweet experience. I relived many breakthrough moments in schools, and the satisfaction of belonging to the thoughtful Middle Start team. But, as I began to update the research after a break of 5 years, I was dismayed that CSR, a vibrant movement until 2005, is reduced to a set of archived reports and websites, and important agencies and coalitions that nurtured that process have ceased to exist. The "what" and the "why" of that progression are narrated here in some detail. However, the emphasis of this chapter is the educational partnership between schools, coaches, districts, regional partners, and government agencies; how it evolved; and what it made possible. Definitely, there were challenges, and I dwell on those as well. In the final analysis, public and private partners play critical roles in conducting, scaling up, and sustaining a good reform. In the case of Middle Start, and the larger field of CSR, one decision to stop funding CSR on the part of the government led to the gradual dismantling of most of the infrastructure upon which the school-level reform rested. Although Middle Start and the other models continue to work with schools on meaningful change, the holistic and long-term pathway established by CSR could not be sustained without government support.

The first section of the chapter briefly summarizes the literature on the need for, and the main goals of, middle-grades reform, and segues into its intersection with CSR. This section also introduces the goals and key components of Middle Start. The second section discusses Owen Middle School (OMS), set in a small city in Michigan, which was a grantee and partner of Middle Start, to elaborate on the reform process at the school level. The third section looks at school districts' perspectives on their role in an educational partnership such as Middle Start; and the fourth section describes the composition, activities, and roles of the Middle Start partnership in Michigan, highlighting the preparation and activities of coaches.

WHY THE MIDDLE GRADES?

In addition to the challenges of providing an academic environment which is engaging, productive, and enriching, educators involved with children facing early adolescence (of ages 11–14) are faced with the issue of supporting their rapidly changing psychosocial development in an appropriate manner. Students' academic interests and needs at this stage are closely integrated with their developmental and social experiences, according to the National Forum to Accelerate Middle-Grades Reform, which is composed of 60 key organizations engaged in middle-grades reform.[4] Additionally, research shows that students' experiences in the middle grades influence their high school graduation and readiness for college. The years a student spends in the middle grades are the best time to identify academic challenges and provide comprehensive support. Balfanz (2009), an expert on middle-grades reform, writes:

> In high-poverty neighborhoods, in particular, our research and school improvement work indicate that students' middle grades experiences have tremendous impact on the extent to which they will close achievement gaps, graduate from high school, and be prepared for college. Consequently, there is a need to rethink the role the middle grades play in the public education system. The middle grades, broadly defined as fifth through eighth grade, need to be seen as the launching pad for a secondary and post-secondary education system that enables all students to obtain the schooling and/or career training they will need to fully experience the opportunities of 21stcentury America.

In order to prepare students to be lifelong learners ready for "college, career, and citizenship," the National Forum (n.d.) seeks to make all middle-grades schools academically excellent, developmentally responsive, and socially equitable. Thus, while educational reform may typically focus on academic indicators, middle-grades reform pushes for equal attention to developmental and social issues. The vision statement is reproduced in Box 3.1 (National Forum to Accelerate Middle-Grades Educational Reform, n.d.):

BOX 3.1

Vision Statement

High-performing schools with middle grades are academically excellent. They challenge all students to use their minds well, providing them with the curriculum, instruction, assessment, support, and time they need to meet rigorous academic standards. They recognize that early adolescence is characterized by dramatic cognitive growth, which enables students to think in more abstract and complex ways. The curriculum and extra-curricular programs in such schools are challenging and engaging, tapping young adolescents' boundless energy, interests, and curiosity. Students learn to understand important concepts, develop essential skills, and apply what they learn to real-world problems. Adults in these schools maintain a rich academic environment by working with colleagues in their schools and communities to deepen their own knowledge and improve their practice.

High-performing schools with middle grades are developmentally responsive. Such schools create small learning communities of adults and students in which stable, close, and mutually respectful relationships support all students' intellectual, ethical, and social growth. They provide comprehensive services to foster healthy physical and emotional development. Students have opportunity for both independent inquiry and learning in cooperation with others. They have time to be reflective and numerous opportunities to make decisions about their learning. Developmentally responsive schools involve families as partners in the education of their children. They welcome families, keep them well informed, help them develop their expectations and skills to support learning, and assure their participation in decision-making. These schools are deeply rooted in their communities. Students have opportunities for active citizenship. They use the community as a classroom, and community members provide resources, connections, and active support.

High-performing schools with middle grades are socially equitable. They seek to keep their students' future options open. They have high expectations for all their students and are committed to helping each child produce work of high quality. These schools make sure that all students are in academically rigorous classes staffed by experienced and expertly prepared teachers. These teachers acknowledge and honor their students' histories and cultures. They work to educate every child well and to overcome systematic variation in resources and outcomes related to race, class, gender, and ability. They engage their communities in supporting all students' learning and growth.

The CSR movement found a ready partner in the middle-grades educational reform movement, as integrated approaches to education reform drove both their agendas. Middle-grades educational reform, first initiated in the 1970s, faced a tension between academic excellence and developmental responsiveness, as some experts felt that the latter was gaining at the expense of the former, resulting in diluted academic rigor in middle-grades schools (Jackson & Davis, 2000; Lipsitz, Mizell, Jackson, & Austin, 1997). In the 1990s, the middle-grades movement struggled to integrate structures that were developmentally appropriate with content that was academically enriching and engaging (Juvonen, Le, Kaganoff, Augustine, & Constant, 2004; Jackson & Davis, 2000; Lee, Smith, Perry, & Smylie, 1999). Thus, structural reforms such as small learning communities of teachers and students (to promote a sense of belonging and support) and grade-level teacher teams (that allowed teachers to coordinate better on teaching and student support) came together with content reforms such as project and other practice-based approaches, theme-based learning, and cooperative learning, that research showed were age appropriate in the middle grades (Jackson & Davis, 2000, pp. 1–3).

However, research on implementation showed that many innovations lacked school-wide acceptance and did not sustain at a level of quality that resulted in improved learning and development for students (Jackson & Davis, 2000; Kasak, 2004). CSR gained prominence in the early 2000s as a way to address issues of quality and scale in school improvement. Aladjem and Borman (2006), experts on CSR, write:

> *Over the past 15 years, comprehensive school reform (CSR) has emerged as a key instantiation of the "whole-school" approach to reform. CSR generally involves school-level adoption and implementation of externally developed, research-based school reform models and approaches. While no exact count exists, data suggest that CSR has been tried in thousands of schools nationwide.*

WHY COMPREHENSIVE SCHOOL REFORM?

There is extensive literature on CSR and the larger field of the processes and approaches of school improvement. CSR gained traction in the 1990s as a promising approach to improving high-poverty, low-performing schools (Slavin & Fashola, 1998; Stringfield & Datnow, 1998;

Herman, Aladjem, McMahon, Masem, Mulligan, Smith, et al., 1999). The NCLB Act, the Bush-era educational policy that dominated the 2000s, provided opportunities for schools to partner with CSR programs and engage in a multiyear process of structural and instructional changes aimed at improving teaching and learning (Borman, Hewes, Overman, & Brown, 2003). Tushnet and Harris (2006) write:

> *Comprehensive school reform is both a concept for an approach to school improvement...and a federal program that provides funds for schools to adopt scientifically-based strategies that cover curriculum, instruction, school organization, and parent involvement. ... The unique aspect of this program, relative to other Title I[5] and the Improving America's Schools Act, was the expectation that schools would collaborate with expert partners to implement whole-school reform methods and strategies with a strong research base and a successful replication record. (pp. 57–58)*

A remarkable achievement of CSR was that it garnered bipartisan support in the United States, as educators and legislators favoring both progressive and traditional approaches found it an appropriate vehicle for improving public school. It grew from an experimental approach, launched in 1991 by New American Schools (see Bodilly, 1996, 1998), to a national pilot in the form of the Comprehensive School Reform Demonstration (CSRD) in 1998, and then became part of federal law in 2000. The NCLB Act (United States Department of Education, 2000), defines CSR as follows:

Components of a Comprehensive School Reform Program

A CSR program is one that addresses each of the following eleven components in a comprehensive and integrated design:

Proven methods and strategies based on scientifically based research: A CSR program employs proven strategies and methods for student learning, teaching, and school management that are based on scientifically based research and effective practices and have been replicated successfully in schools.

Component one emphasizes the need for schools in designing their CSR to employ proven strategies and methods that are grounded in scientifically based research in core academic subjects, especially mathematics and reading. Staying focused on academic achievement, building a comprehensive program that supports it, and emphasizing "what works" in the classroom are important elements of a successful comprehensive design.

Comprehensive design: A comprehensive design for effective school functioning integrates instruction, assessment, classroom management, professional development, parental involvement, and school management. By addressing needs identified through a school needs assessment, it aligns the school's curriculum, technology, and professional development into a plan for school-wide change. The ultimate goal of this design is to enable all students to meet challenging State content and student academic achievement standards.

Professional development: The program provides high-quality and continuous teacher and staff professional development and training. The professional development involves proven innovative strategies that are both cost-effective and easily accessible and ensures that teachers are able to use State assessments and challenging State academic content standards to improve instructional practice and student academic achievement.

Well-designed professional development activities increase all teachers' knowledge of both the academic subjects they teach and effective instructional strategies that are grounded in scientifically based research. They include strategies such as partnerships with institutions of higher education and address topics such as the use of data and assessment, the use of technology, and improving the instruction of special needs children.

This professional development is intensive, sustained over time, and classroom focused. Those who participate in professional development also help to design it, and the design is well integrated with school and district educational improvement plans. The professional development component is regularly evaluated to gauge its impact on increased teacher effectiveness and improved achievement. Strategies employed are consistent with high-quality professional development as described in Title II, Part A of the Elementary and Secondary Education Act (ESEA).

Measurable goals and benchmarks: A CSR program includes measurable goals for student academic achievement and establishes benchmarks for meeting those goals. The Department encourages Local Education Agencies (LEAs) to link these goals to the State's definition of adequate yearly progress (AYP) in Section 1111(b)(2) of the ESEA.

Support within the school: Teachers, principals, administrators, and other staff throughout the school support the program in a CSR school. They demonstrate this support by, among other activities, understanding and embracing the school's comprehensive reform program, focusing on continuous improvement of classroom instruction, and participating in professional development.

Support for teachers and principals: A CSR program provides support for teachers, principals, administrators, and other school staff by creating shared leadership and a broad base of responsibility for reform efforts. The program encourages teamwork and the celebration of accomplishments. These and other means of support are part of the school's comprehensive design.

Parental and community involvement: The program provides for the meaningful involvement of parents and the local community in planning, implementing, and evaluating school improvement activities. In addressing this component, schools create strategies that are consistent with the parental involvement requirements of Title I, Part A. (See section 1118 of the ESEA.) Schools pay special attention to building parents' capacity for involvement and design ways in which parents can be brought into the instructional program and contribute to the academic achievement of their children.

External technical support and assistance: The program uses high-quality external support and assistance from an entity that has experience and expertise in school-wide reform and improvement, which may include an institution of higher education. The CSR legislation requires that State Educational Agencies(SEAs) ensure that funded programs are supported by qualified technical assistance providers that have a successful track record, financial stability, the capacity to deliver high-quality materials, professional development for school personnel, and on-site support during the full implementation period of the reform.

Annual evaluation: The program ensures accountability by including a plan for the annual evaluation of the implementation of school reforms and the student results achieved. The evaluation helps ensure that the school is making progress towards achieving its measurable goals and benchmarks and that necessary adjustments and improvements will be made to the reform strategies.

Coordination of resources: The comprehensive program must identify Federal, State, local and private financial and other resources that schools can use to coordinate services that support and sustain comprehensive school reform.

Strategies that improve academic achievement: The program must meet one of the following requirements: the program has been found, through scientifically based research, to significantly improve the academic achievement of participating students; or the program has been found to have strong evidence that it will significantly improve the academic achievement of participating children.

Using all eleven components, schools must create a comprehensive, integrated reform program that affects all subjects, all teachers, and all children in the school.

Scientifically based research and research-based practices are terms in the NCLB Act that fuelled heated debates on what is and is not scientific, and who decides the issue. The Act defined scientific research narrowly as randomized experiments that can establish a causal link between a particular practice and gains in student achievement on standardized tests in comparison to a "control" group. The National Research Council published guidelines on scientific research in education in 2002 (National Research Council, 2002) that deemed nonexperimental research uniformly unscientific. Their approach did not take into account the considerable limitations of randomized experiments in education research or provide alternative methods of studying CSR programs and selecting appropriate reform practices. See Howe (2004) for a strong critique of randomized experiments and their use in CSR research.

The evolving CSR movement crystallized between the late 1990s and early 2000s when the U.S. Department of Education nominated the Northwest Regional Educational Laboratory to review a varied set of CSR models and nominate the most effective models in their Catalog of School Reform Models[6] (the first edition was published in 1998). Middle Start was included as an effective model in the 2004 edition of the Catalog, which became an influential reference for states and districts for selection of CSR models.

In the following paragraphs, I discuss how Middle Start worked on comprehensive middle-grades reform with one school in Michigan over a 4-year period. Owen Middle School (OMS) is located in a small city in Michigan; it has over 500 students, 50 percent of which are eligible for free or reduced-price lunch.[7] Owen worked with Middle Start for over four years, both through its interactions with a Middle Start coach as well as participation in networking activities organized by the MMSP.

The following section briefly describes the evolution of Middle Start, before describing the partnership between the school and the model.

MIDDLE START

As stated earlier, Middle Start began in 1994 with 12 schools in Michigan and grew into a national effort that reached over 100 schools by 2004. The WKKF was the primary sponsor, and in the late 1990s, Middle Start qualified for inclusion in CSRD, the pilot for the CSR section of the NCLB Act. In 2000, the Foundation for the Mid South and AED began an effort similar to the initiative in Michigan in Arkansas, Louisiana, and Mississippi. In 2004, Middle Start qualified for CSR funds, which boosted the national implementation of the model. However, by the end of 2005, the CSR program, despite showing promise, lost its funding due to strain on federal budgets brought about by the war in Iraq. A press release from the Coalition for Comprehensive School Improvement (CCSI) dated December 22, 2005, marks the stoppage of funding for CSR on account of the elimination of the program from the budget of NCLB:[8]

> *Today, federal lawmakers voted to terminate all grants to schools for the Comprehensive School Reform program. It's estimated more than 1,000 of the nation's most needy schools will lose ongoing federal grants for school improvement efforts. Congress first authorized the CSR program in 1998 with bi-partisan support, and because of the program's strong performance, lawmakers included it as part of the No Child Left Behind Act in 2001. Federal funding for CSR has fluctuated between $205 million and $310 million since the inception of the program. Today's vote eliminates all CSR grants to schools, retaining only eight million dollars for national activities, making it one of the largest reductions to a single education program this year.*

The index page of the website of the Middle Start National Center (n.d.) describes the four principles of the program:

> *Middle Start is a nationally recognized program of the Academy for Educational Development dedicated to improving teaching and learning and ensuring academic success and healthy development*

*for every middle-grades student. With over a decade of experi-
ence, Middle Start helps schools develop the characteristics of
high performing middle-grades schools:*

- *Academically challenging environments that support the
  diverse needs of ALL learners.*
- *Personalized learning communities informed by the stages of
  young adolescent development.*
- *Reflective review and self-assessment to ensure continuous
  improvement.*
- **Collaborative leadership committed to family and community
  partnerships to sustain success.*

The following three sections discuss the school-based work, district
relationships, and the coaches' network, a part of the MMSP.

SCHOOL-BASED WORK

OMS[9] is a typical American middle school that includes grades 6,7, and
8. It is located in a small city in eastern Michigan, with great diversity
in the cultural and socioeconomic make up of its citizens. I spent four
years conducting a qualitative study of OMS, where I visited the school
on a quarterly basis from 1998 through 2002, and interacted with faculty, students, some parents, and community members. I conducted
interviews with all the groups and observed classrooms on all my visits.
On some visits, I shadowed students for part of their day and spent time
at the lunchroom and at their co-curricular activities. I also coordinated
some of my visits with that of their Middle Start coach, Nancy Spencer,
in order to observe her work with the school over time. I chose Owen as
the school-level example in this book because I felt that its experiences
during its work with Middle Start exemplify what a school can achieve
in a few years. Again, it is the pursuit of the question—"Why does what
works work?"—which drives this chapter. Instead of dwelling on challenges and weaknesses of an approach, I focus on understanding the
complexity inherent in school improvement and figuring out what will
advance teaching and learning.

At the time of the study, Owen had about 500 students, half of whom
were Caucasian, 40 percent African-American, and a small percentage
were Latino and Asian. Over half the students were identified as belonging

to lower-income households, and qualified for free or reduced-price lunch. About 20 percent were identified as having special needs. The staff at Owen had an impressive average of 14-years teaching experience overall, and the school had a teacher:pupil ratio of 1:30 on average.

Edna Manning was the principal of Owen during the time of the study. Edna and the staff of Owen were very open to the idea of Middle Start working with the building, and a grant from WKKF in 1997, as part of the early initiatives of Middle Start, started off the process. The school continued to work with Middle Start after it was awarded a CSR grant by the state department. Owen was thus actively involved with Middle Start from 1997 through 2002. The Middle Start school improvement coach at Owen, Dr Nancy Spencer, a University professor and a veteran teacher educator, worked with the school on a weekly basis on goal-setting, planning, implementation, self-assessment, and professional development. These aspects are discussed in detail in this section.[10]

The school had an inviting layout with each group of classrooms set around a "commons," a spacious and colorful space filled with student work and motivational posters. During one of my visits, a local jazz band held a concert for each house in the commons. Each commons led to a courtyard with gardens, which the students maintained. One garden housed a "weather station," where students recorded the temperature and monitored weather conditions.

Teachers and the coach alike described Owen's principal, Edna Manning, as a leader with a vision, who encouraged staff to take initiative. Manning began her work at Owen in 1996. The coach, district representative, and some staff noted that the school had a poor climate and poor test scores when Manning began, and by all estimates, instruction, climate, and student outcomes improved under her stewardship. The coach characterized Manning as a strong leader who "manages, listens, reads, wants to know what the best strategies are—she's an instructional leader." Manning, in turn, emphasized that she "could not have achieved all this without Middle Start. Middle Start is a blessing!" She said that she was new at Owen when she began the partnership with Middle Start and was faced with a demoralized staff and a poor academic environment. Through their partnership, Manning and Spencer were able to win over the staff, by convincing the board to support interdisciplinary teaming[11] and sanction time and money for professional development for teachers in important aspects of middle-grades-appropriate curriculum and instruction. The school was also able to win a CSR grant to implement Middle Start, which helped Owen further advance its efforts. Manning noted that Spencer, the Middle Start coach, was an "invaluable guide" to her.

The principal and teachers, after much discussion and analysis of school and student data with the help of Spencer, decided that their Middle Start initiative would focus on literacy and enhancement of reading and writing across the curriculum. I interviewed the district officials overseeing Owen on an annual basis. My point person became the district curriculum director, Lisa Brown, who said that she was happy that Owen's plans were aligned with "the district's emphasis on reading and writing." The district also provided the extra staff needed to make teaming possible in all the houses, demonstrating its support of Owen's restructuring efforts. At the end of the fourth year of implementation, she too noted significant improvements in students' academic work and in Owen's overall school climate.

Middle Start coaches were the primary link between the MMSP and Middle Start schools. They engaged in workshops and in meetings of MMSP to build their capacity to coach Middle Start schools. Their preparation included capacity building in the area of data analysis, leadership development, awareness of curricular and instructional strategies and programs, and approaches for reflection on and evaluation of the quality and outcomes of the implementation. Coaches wrote monthly logs on their activities and participated in monthly meetings where they reflected on their work, learned new skills and concepts, and also learned about what was happening in other Middle Start schools. Studies of Middle Start coaching show that coaches varied greatly in style and efficacy. However, the majority of coaches played the role of "guide on the side," rather than a more directive role. They coached staff to make joint decisions, helped them identify priorities and maintain their focus, and aim for a high level of implementation (see Gopalan & Jessup, 2001, for a detailed discussion of school-based coaching). Thus, understanding the role that Spencer played in Owen's Middle Start implementation is critical.

As mentioned, Dr Nancy Spencer, a veteran in the field of teacher preparation and a professor at a nearby university, first established relationships with middle schools, including Owen, in her school district in 1996. As a representative of her university, she joined the MMSP in 1997 and began her work as a Middle Start coach in that same year at Owen. With WKKF's backing and the school district's support, she began the first steps of "setting goals and building trust among teachers," through ongoing discussions and awareness sessions. Spencer also helped the staff at Owen apply for the CSR grant in 1999, and this grant enabled the school to continue working with Middle Start for three more years. Both Manning and Spencer described Spencer's work at Owen as wide ranging: She provided in-services for Owen staff on working as effective teams, demonstrated varied instructional strategies, introduced staff to varied student assessment strategies, and guided the staff in selecting appropriate professional development in the area of literacy-across-the-curriculum. As part of MMSP, she was able to draw on other partners' areas of expertise and experiences in schools to boost Owen's efforts. Manning described their working style, thus: "I share with her the direction I would like the school to go, and she shares her expertise and helps us get the resources we need."A teacher in the school described Spencer as: "a guide for the school, and an advocate for teachers and students." Several staff also described Spencer as an effective professional developer. A few teams in the school said that they needed more time with Spencer as a team to learn more about effective teaming as well as to show her what they were already doing. In Spencer's estimate, Owen made significant progress in developing a socially nurturing environment for students, as well as a richer, more varied academic program. She said:

> Owen is a real different school compared to five years ago. My strategy has been to ask them what they want to get accomplished and when they identify what this is, to get them the resources they need to go ahead and do it. First we worked on teaming, and when we got that right, we've started chipping away at instructional practices. That's the focus now, to improve instruction school-wide.

What follows is a detailed description of Owen's Middle Start implementation. The majority of staff reported that they were "excited" or "have come a long way" from where they were five years ago through implementing teaming, inclusion, and Core Explore[12]—three major structural changes that the school conducted in partnership with Spencer and Middle Start. The same staff also noted that classroom practices had moved significantly in the direction of project-based education, including teamwork and the use of educational technology. Staff offered considerable additional academic support for students through special programs such as Core Explore, after school tutoring, and the homework hotline. Efforts to improve the school climate and provide support for students were undertaken simultaneously. The staff welcomed parents and community members into the school through free health services offered by their health center, an orientation for parents of incoming sixth graders, student-led parent–teacher conferences, a parent newsletter featuring student work, and team–parent meetings during team planning time. Eighth-grade staff also incorporated career education and an orientation to the local high school to prepare their students for the next phase of their education.

Structural Changes

Among the main structural changes were the development of a strong school leadership team and grade-level houses and teams, inclusion of special education students in teams, and changes in the schedule to accommodate common planning time for teachers and additional learning time (Core Explore) for students. The coach, in addition to working with a leadership team to get the school board's support for teaming, also guided the development of teaming with inclusion at Owen and pushed the school to create additional learning time for students. Spencer, Manning, and the school leadership team envisioned these structural changes as fostering a developmentally responsive environment for students and supporting academic innovation and improvement. Almost all staff (including those who felt that there were too many changes) felt that the school had evolved through these structures into a more supportive environment for students. The coach agreed stating, "You'll see a very nurturing school," but added that the staff needed to "embrace the structures philosophically rather than just physically," in order for their potential to be fully realized.

The school leadership team, or the school improvement team, was composed of staff representing the different grade levels. The principal described this team as the group she brainstormed with and as "spokespeople" for new ideas among the staff. The school leadership team had revolving leadership—for example, on every visit, the team was led by a new staff member. All new staff members served on leadership team in their first year at Owen so that they quickly became familiar with the goals of the schools and related efforts to accomplish them. The principal's rationale was that the school was involved in a large change effort and new staff needed to understand it and become a part of it. She said:

When there's someone new, the first step is that they become a part of the school improvement team. That's a must for the first year, in order to be a part of the (Middle Start) process. As a teacher, you're so overwhelmed with so many things that you don't know why you are doing what you are doing.

The principal also noted that this approach both oriented new teachers to the larger effort the school was in and ensured that the latter was sustained, in spite of changes in staff. I met the chair of the leadership team, a young woman beginning her teaching career, who described the leadership team as an entity that prioritized areas for implementation and sought to build consensus on how to proceed with implementation:

We [the leadership team] seek to set and attain school-wide goals. We consider school and student data in light of our goals. Our emphasis this year is literacy as we found that students read fictional but not informational text well. We then identify professional development based on thinking through our goals.

Teaming was the most extensive structural innovation that the school undertook as part of Middle Start. Teaming is a core principle of middle-grades educational reform and has persisted for over two decades of the middle-grades movement, as it has demonstrated its ability when implemented well, to provide a nurturing environment for students as well as improve academic engagement (Casas, 2011). Owen's teaming practices developed over a period of four years and incorporated several of the practices recommended in the literature on teaming. Owen had three grade levels—sixth, seventh, and eighth—each composed of two teams. Each team consisted of four teachers from Math, Science, Social Studies, and English. Each grade level also had a student counselor, who worked closely with both grade-level teams. The daily schedule was revised to include common planning time for each team to meet several times a week. These meetings were critical to the functioning of the team, as they allowed for teams to work together on integrated curricular projects, discuss students' needs and challenges, address parent concerns as a team, and understand patterns in students' performance on assessments across different subject areas. Working together as a team thus afforded teachers an opportunity to understand each student's aptitudes and challenges better, as well as design and carry out in-depth learning projects that cut across the curriculum.

Implementing teaming in all the grades required additional funds. Half of the cost of the additional staff needed for teaming was provided by the WKKF for the first two years. The school district, after studying the ways in which Owen's teams functioned, assumed the costs of supporting teaming with common planning time at Owen thereafter. The funds for extensive professional development from the CSR grant helped teams use their flexible schedule and team-planning time effectively. The majority of teachers at Owen stated that teaming helped them become a cohesive decision-making unit, allowing them to support each other instructionally, and develop consistent rules and expectations for students across a grade-level house. Teachers said:

When I'm doing a project with my class, the team [seventh grade] knows about it. We understand and support what the others on the team are doing.

Teaming is the reorganization of the school to provide an environment of learning. There is consistency in rules, regulations, and expectations all across the eighth grade house.

Although students do not specifically refer to teaming, several of them noticed that their teachers' expectations for work and behavior were consistent across the team. Each house has a counselor, connected to both grade-level teams in the house. Students mentioned the counselor as an adult they could talk with about personal and academic difficulties. The coach, district liaison, principal, and staff all described teaming as "well in place." The instructional aspects of teaming are discussed in a following section titled "Classroom Practices."

Core Explore was designed by the Middle Start coach to provide students with additional learning time during which they completed outstanding assignments, did work for extra credit, and engaged in enrichment activities. Students were divided into small groups that interacted closely with a teacher as they participated in the aforementioned activities. The program was popular with students and staff alike. Students felt they were able to keep up with their work better and get the attention they needed from the teacher. Teachers felt they had a chance to interact with students in smaller groups and understand their needs well.

Inclusion of special education students in regular education was a major thrust of Owen's change efforts. Structurally, this was accomplished through teaming, as each team included subject area teachers and a teacher consultant with expertise in inclusion. In the principal's estimate, one half of the students in special education attended classes with other students for most or all of their subject-area classes by the end of the grant period.[13] The teacher consultant worked with the subject teacher to provide appropriate intensive help to students who needed it. The other half of students in special education went to elective classes with the other students, but remained in self-contained classes the rest of the time. The support provided by the teacher consultant, the additional learning time provided by Core Explore every day, as well as the exposure to differentiated instruction for teachers are factors that the principal and coach see as fostering equitable learning opportunities for students of varied learning abilities.

Classroom Practices

Classrooms at Owen were usually abuzz with activity. Students were seen working in pairs and small groups on projects, engaging in animated discussions with the teacher about a topic, conducting Internet searches for a paper, reading and writing independently, and listening to the teacher read or explain a new topic from a text. Project-based education was a major mode of learning at Owen: Students, with the teacher's guidance, learned subject-area content through individual or team projects and produced scripts, essays, models, and other products after a period of research on the topic. An article in the school magazine describes the culminating project for a rainforest theme, where students put together a mini rainforest in their common area, with different kinds of trees, animals, and birds found in the rainforest.

Literacy-across-the-curriculum was evident in the majority of classes. Teachers required students to use varied language skills to produce projects, including simple tasks such as tests of vocabulary, reading excerpts from their texts, or involved in activities such as text-based discussions, book and scriptwriting, Internet searches, and poster making. Students also performed their plays and displayed their posters and books in exhibitions and open houses for parents. Such activities were in abundance in Social Science, Science, and Language arts classes, but not present in Math classes. In a seventh-grade Science class, for example, the teacher and students were engrossed in a discussion of the conversion of potential energy to kinetic energy. In a fast-flowing discussion, they debated the forms of energy described in their text in context of examples they were familiar with, such as a rocket launch, a tree's reliance on the sun's energy, and the production of heat and sound energy when playing a musical instrument. In another seventh-grade Social Science class, students presented informational posters on a country of their choice. Each student displayed a poster of the country's name, a picture of the flag, demographic data, languages, modes of dress, main exports and imports, and major historical events. Students' writing is also showcased in a monthly school newsletter, which is sent to staff and community members.

Manning emphasized that literacy-across-the-curriculum was the greatest emphasis in the school in the 2002 school year. She also stated that teachers would undertake further professional development in incorporating cooperative learning, newer approaches to assessment, career education, and technology in instruction as the year progressed. She described the school's priority as "deepening instructional areas" in the last year of the CSR grant.

Students' work was displayed throughout the school, demonstrating students' perspectives on current events, their imaginative writing, as well as cross-disciplinary assignments. However, several teachers and the principal noted that they were still learning how to "map the curriculum well, and develop truly interdisciplinary units."

The majority of students were enthusiastic about their classes. An eighth grader who had started in the sixth grade at Owen said that she saw improvement on several fronts in the school:

Teachers are more helpful and class activities are better. There is more group work, more kids participate in class.

Two sixth graders stated:

The "funner" they make it, the easier it [content] is to get.
Every teacher makes their class fun and interesting. They grab your attention.

Project-based education included projects large and small, which students created as they explored content in greater depth. I noted simple projects, such as three-dimensional, colored shapes, that sixth graders created in Math class to explore the characteristics of cubes, pyramids, and other shapes. Students painted designs on the shapes and hung them with string, creating a colorful display on the ceiling of their classroom. I also observed complex projects, such as a flipbook that seventh-grade students created as part of a science project exploring eight stages of the repopulation of an island devastated by a volcano. The assignment asked students to write the book from the viewpoint of a spider, the first creature to reappear on the island. For extra credit in the same class, students could create an illustrated alphabet book organized by names of animals which identified their predators and prey. I heard from an eighth-grade teacher about a long-term science project in which students tested for radon in their homes, prepared a report and an oral presentation including visual aids (a poster or a set of overheads), and compiled a fact sheet for the larger public on radon.

Overwhelmingly, students supported "learning by doing" and said they had opportunities to learn this way several times a week. They also said they liked to "work in groups"—it helped them learn better. A seventh grader said, "I love science. It's exciting when you can look through a microscope and learn about the organism that you read about in your book!" An eighth grader remarked: "I learn a lot in groups, except when I need to learn alone. I do a lot of work in groups in science. For math, mostly alone."

School Climate and Social Supports

Students listed their involvement in several activities around the school, access to counselors, orientations for sixth graders, and great health services within the school as positive aspects of the school.

Student involvement in school activities included working in the school garden, manning the weather station, and writing for the school newsletter. Students proudly showed off the trees and flowers they took care of. In the courtyard, two seventh graders described their love of working outdoors and watching things bloom, and showed us the tulips that they had planted the previous fall that were blooming when we visited in spring. In one courtyard, a group of eighth graders collected data from the weather station, with one reading the temperature, another reading the wind direction (measured by the speed of rotations of plastic pots tied to an old bike wheel), and a third recording both. Students compiled this information everyday and presented it over the intercom to the entire school. The school's newsletter was choc a bloc with students' essays, poems, and drawings. For example, a seventh grader narrated the sequence of events that led to a visit from a district representative. Students had written to the representative about their concerns regarding pollution, guns and violence, healthcare, and other social issues, as part of a Social Studies project. The student wrote about the interaction between students and the representative when she visited their class.

Counseling was widely mentioned by students as one of the social supports available in the school. The majority of students described their counselor as someone they could go to with personal and academic troubles. I met an eighth grader outside the counselor's office who said he was going to talk to her about difficult times that his family was facing. I spoke with two counselors in the school who emphasized their readiness to support students with questions about high school, careers, as well as peer- or family-related problems. The sixth-grade counselor said: "I am here for students, parents, and teachers."

Orientations at the sixth and eighth grades aimed to prepare students for their next step. The school put together an orientation for incoming sixth graders on the physical features and processes of their new school. A few students reported building a model of the school that would help incoming sixth graders and their parents find their way around the school easily. Similarly, Owen had an orientation for its eighth graders on what to expect in high school, so that they were prepared for the transition better. Eighth-grade teachers described taking their students to visit the high school to help them visualize ninth grade and be better prepared for it. A teacher also described integrating career education for eighth graders, including exposure to a career software package that "helps students determine their interest areas and pick jobs that match their interests."

Parent involvement increased over the years of the implementation due to teaming, according to teachers and the principal. Manning said: "Over 1500 parents have walked through our doors since the beginning of the school year. They are very happy with the restructuring of the school. Our enrolment is up." Teachers in all the grade-level teams reported meeting with parents as a team, usually with the counselor present, to discuss a student's academic or behavioral issues. All teams stated that this presented a "holistic picture" of the student to both the parent as well as teachers. A teacher said: "The parent is not hearing differing accounts of the student from each teacher. A parent can talk with the whole team and see what her child is capable of doing academically." The coach, however, felt that parent involvement needed to change into "true engagement." Her vision was for parents to be involved in "decision-making, in classrooms, and other meaningful avenues" and stated that parent involvement was a priority for her work with the school in the coming year.

Overall, Owen's partnership with Middle Start resulted in concrete improvements in structural arrangements, classroom practices, social supports for students, and school climate. Through engaging teachers, especially new teachers in school leadership activities, and gaining the district's support for interdisciplinary teaming, Owen also put in place a system for sustaining the concepts and structures needed for ongoing reform. In the first two years, Owen established interdisciplinary grade-level teams, and over the next two years, focused on improving teaching and learning through project-based education and writing-across-the-curriculum.

MIDDLE START AND DISTRICTS

While there were qualitative improvements in Owen's teaching and learning environment, and staff's awareness and participation in middle-grades-appropriate practices, the question of sustainability remained at Owen. Partly, the district's heightened awareness of what works in middle-grades education and their support of interdisciplinary teaming were two accomplishments of Middle Start during the five years of its involvement with Owen. Additionally, the MMSP connected Owen with other Middle Start CSRD schools in a regional network that continued to interact with coaches, professional developers, and leadership developers on a monthly basis post the grant period. District leaders were also invited to these networking meetings, as their input and continued support of the school-level efforts was a high priority for Middle Start. District leaders were also impressed with Owen's improvement, and initiated teaming in the other middle school in the district.

Despite the importance of schools and districts being in agreement about middle-grades educational practices, and the district's critical role in sustaining and scaling up effective educational practices, CSR policy has created one-on-one partnerships between schools and providers, largely leaving districts out of the process (Marsh, 2000; U.S. Department of Education, 2000) The Owen study shows that schools require significant district support to launch and sustain the extensive structural and instructional improvements, and this finding is echoed in other literature as well (Hoy & Dipaola, 2009; Spillane, 2000; Elmore & Mclaughlin, 1988). MacIver and Farley (2003) reviewed literature on both sides of the districts debate and concluded that district participation in school reform is a must, especially in large districts, as they are integrally involved in professional development, instructional practices, and student learning. Spillane (2006) strongly argues that districts are essential to systemic reform as only district involvement can ensure that promising educational practices from a small group of schools find their way into an entire system.

Schools with middle grades undertaking CSR are especially affected by this paradox because they rely on districts to hire teachers with middle-grades certification and need district support to implement small learning communities and adopt interdisciplinary instruction and equitable modes of student assignment—keystones of the middle-grades educational reform movement in the United States. However, the CSR grant puts schools and partners in close interaction without involving the district. In this section, I highlight the findings of a three-year study of districts' perspectives on Middle Start's approach that integrating districts more effectively into the school–CSR program partnership is a critical ingredient of long-lasting reform, echoing other researchers who have highlighted this shortcoming of CSR (Tushnet & Harris, 2006; Massell, 2000; Center for Policy Research in Education, 1998). In this section, I also describe the school-district-Middle Start partnership's scope, highlights, shortcomings, and needs.

This study was conducted with district respondents from 13 districts representing 19 schools that received Middle Start CSR grants from 1999 to 2002. They participated in three annual phone interviews (spring 2000, 2001, and 2002) to discuss the role of Middle Start CSR in grantee schools and districts. District respondents included superintendents, assistant superintendents, school improvement coordinators, and coordinators of state and federal programs. The sample included rural and urban districts in Michigan. Ten rural and mid-sized urban districts had one Middle Start CSR grantee school each. Three larger urban districts had two to four Middle Start CSR grantee schools. Fortunately, the sample of district respondents stayed the same over the three years in the 13 districts, enabling good comparisons of the data over time. The interviews probed the extent of districts' awareness, involvement, and support of middle-grades educational reform using the strategies of comprehensive school improvement. The annual interviews tracked changes in respondents' perspectives on issues such as district involvement in Middle Start CSR grant writing, school-level implementation, coaching, monitoring and assessment, sustaining reform, changes in district policies, and K-12 coordination. The interviews accompanied a larger qualitative study of the 19 schools that examined school-based coaching, implementation, and changes in teaching and learning over the same period.

The findings of this study show that the majority of district leaders became highly supportive of Middle Start CSR's work in their middle-grades schools over the three years of implementation despite very little contact with MMSP or the coaches. Respondents noted that CSR was an important initiative both because of the scope of improvement undertaken by schools as well as the sustained involvement of external CSR programs in school-based improvement. District respondents reported that they encouraged schools to select Middle Start, or supported school's own decisions to do the same, because of their commitment to improving middle-grades education in their district. They reported playing close attention to school-based implementation of Middle Start because of their heightened interest in CSR and concern about improving academic outcomes in the middle grades. In most cases, respondents reported minimal contact with Middle Start coaches and other staff and stated that they learned about Middle Start through closely observing school-based implementation through visitations and hearing ongoing reports from principals and teachers regarding professional development and implementation activities. District leaders stated that they continued to stay interested in Middle Start because of the sustained efforts of Middle Start schools to improve instructional and organizational arrangements and encouraging trends in student performance and behavior. In districts with multiple middle-grades schools, district leaders reported elevating Middle Start schools to the position of "demonstration" schools that would guide other middle-grades schools in their reform efforts. The majority of district respondents reported greater commitment to five areas of comprehensive middle-grades reform, including:

1. Addressing the academic and developmental needs of students entering early adolescence.
2. Supporting organizational changes such as interdisciplinary teaming in schools with middle grades.
3. Supporting ongoing teacher collaboration and professional development for instructional improvement.
4. Encouraging partnerships with CSR program staff such as Middle Start coaches and professional development providers.
5. Endorsing comprehensive school reform as a vehicle for school improvement, and implementing coherent rather than piecemeal approaches to school improvement.

District respondents reported concerns with the following:

1. Strengthening collaboration between CSR program staff and district leaders to foster greater collaboration and alignment between their respective initiatives.
2. Aligning CSR program-based professional development with district-initiated professional development and improving professional development in specific areas.

Strengths of School's Participation in Middle Start CSR

Nine of the 13 respondents reported overwhelming support of the comprehensive middle-grades educational reform strategies employed by Middle Start providers and schools. In three urban districts with multiple middle schools, district leaders created opportunities for Middle Start schools to network with non–Middle Start schools in an effort to share new knowledge and skills. Specifically, district leaders reported that districts were better equipped, as a result of monitoring school's participation in Middle Start, to (*a*) help schools address the needs of students entering early adolescence; (*b*) create or improve interdisciplinary teams; (*c*) support professional development for teachers; (*d*) encourage partnerships with externally developed programs; and (*e*) endorse comprehensive school reform.

Address the needs of students in the middle grades

All 13 district leaders discussed the importance of district-level awareness of the academic and developmental needs of students in the middle grades. In the first year, 7 of 13 leaders reported that Middle Start had helped them better understand students entering early adolescence and make a commitment to restructuring middle-grades education to address students' needs. By the third year, 10 district leaders reported extensive efforts in Middle Start CSR schools to implement age-appropriate instructional and organizational improvements, and stated that districts would continue to support such improvement past the grant period. A superintendent stated:

We've moved from a junior high to a middle school mindset. The three-year process allows us to think differently about the education of pre-adolescents. Middle Start has given us a good foundation. The mindset has improved and staff is aware and looking for improved strategies to help students.

Another superintendent noted:

The achievement of Middle Start is that it has won seasoned staff over. There is a greater awareness of kids in the middle grades. There is a significant change in how we are taking into account CSR and Middle Start when planning district middle level programs.

Create or improve interdisciplinary teams

Eleven of the 13 district leaders emphasized the contributions of inter-disciplinary teams to improved teacher collaboration and instructional improvement and stated that they would continue to support the staffing requirements of teaming and common planning time for teams despite financial constraints. District leaders noted that interdisciplinary teams were initiated early in the first year of Middle Start CSR and that they had made substantial strides in improving school climate and instructional practices by the third year. A district coordinator of federal and state programs stated:

Based on conversations with kids, parents and teachers, I feel classrooms are more sensitive to students. Teachers are better aware of the issues that impact their learning and interactions, and handle situations more effectively by working as a team. There is greater understanding of the changes in developmental stages of the child in sixth, seventh and eighth grade. ...The district will sustain this approach. It's a matter of continuing and facilitating initiatives.

A superintendent stated:

Teaming has led to student achievement. Collaboration and communication among teachers is critical as collegiality capitalizes on teachers' strengths. Students benefit from teaming.

Support professional development for teachers

When discussing implementation of Middle Start at the school level, all 13 respondents highlighted the importance of professional development in bringing about structural and instructional improvements at the school level. The majority of respondents stated that professional development in teaming and instructional areas such as thematic instruction, curriculum alignment, differentiated instruction, and cooperative learning had helped teachers develop a broader repertoire. Overall, district leaders reported high levels of satisfaction with professional development facilitated by Middle Start providers and supported teacher participation in professional development. A coordinator of state and federal programs noted:

Instructionally the culture is changing from "I taught it, they didn't get it" to "I taught it, why didn't they get it?" This word [why] changes the culture of education. Teachers are looking at data and asking why. Middle Start has facilitated changes at the middle level.

A superintendent stated:

Teachers doing a bad job are being shown up by teaming. Teams have worked to create a good learning environment—a family— instead of piecemeal, individual classrooms. Staff reactions are positive about what is happening in classroom. These are indicators to me that student learning is improving. Teachers have had professional development in developmental responsiveness and are more aware of it.

Respondents also expressed commitment to sustaining professional development for middle-grades teachers at high levels after the period of the CSR grant through drawing from other funding streams. They stated that districts would reallocate funds, align initiatives, and raise funds through grant-writing to sustain professional development at the higher levels supported by schools' CSR grants. A superintendent stated:

We will maintain and sustain professional development through combining our Title I, Eisenhower and Title 6 funds. Our district has made a strong commitment.

A district coordinator for school improvement said:

We are working with the school to use CSR and district money to institutionalize and sustain professional development. It [Middle Start CSR] has brought to our attention that for the core of a building to change it takes 5 years. A building that qualifies for CSR is not a building on the verge of excellence. People need to identify the concerns, build dialogue, plan, and take ownership. It takes more than three years.

Encourage partnerships with externally developed programs

The majority of district leaders also reported higher levels of satisfaction with Middle Start coaches and professional development providers over the three years of implementation and stated that their experience with Middle Start had disposed them favorably to outside experts collaborating with their schools as they saw them as bringing "new blood" into the system. Nine of 13 respondents were very positive in their assessment of Middle Start program staff and stated that they would encourage schools to develop long-term partnerships with external experts. Two district leaders mentioned efforts to identify district funds to pay for an additional year of coaching from Middle Start after the three-year CSR grant. A coordinator of state and federal programs stated:

External people who come in to look and say "Hey this is what I see" are very important. ... [Middle Start coach] provides good services. ... Every building knows who he is and what he does. He is a part of it. ... We need outside funding sources and outside expertise on how to move forward.

A district coordinator of school improvement said:

Our [Middle Start] coaches are very approachable, professional, connected to other schools and districts, and bring valuable information with them.

Endorse comprehensive school reform

All 13 respondents stated that Middle Start schools' experiments with comprehensive school reform demonstrated that systematic and well-coordinated reform efforts could bring about meaningful improvements for students in a few years. Several respondents said that previous district initiatives had used "one-shot interventions" or "piecemeal approaches" that required a significant investment of funds and effort but had not benefited students. They also emphasized that school improvement is a process requiring at least a few years of sustained work, and that previous initiatives had failed because they had not considered the complexity of school reform. A superintendent said:

> *Comprehensive school reform is about different strands that have a common purpose—the success of each student. It takes a school 3–5 years to transform. I always knew that school improvement is a complex phenomenon but this [Middle Start] school gives you a living example. There was targeted and meaningful staff development, so it's no surprise to me. We have to put a new system into place.*

A coordinator of federal and state programs stated:

> *CSR has forced districts to learn to coordinate resources better. We're looking at comprehensive school reform to help students by considering how different strands of effort can come together as a coherent whole, focused on the students who need them most. Middle Start has brought greater cohesiveness to our efforts through addressing teaming, block schedule, using data. ...I really believe that CSR has been a catalyst for our buildings.*

Concerns with School's Participation in Middle Start CSR

Some district respondents expressed an interest in strengthening the collaboration between program staff and district representatives to ease barriers to school improvement at the building level, as well as in aligning program-based and district-initiated professional development and improving professional development in the area of inclusion. In general, they recommended that Middle Start develop a stronger relationship with the district so that it could better guide and support school-level efforts in the long term.

Strengthen program–district collaboration

The majority of district respondents stated that they had minimal contact with Middle Start program staff because coaches and professional development providers were contracted to work primarily at the school level. They emphasized the importance of improved communication and collaboration between districts and CSR program staff, as it would fall on the district to support ongoing capacity building and school improvement at the school level. Three of 13 district providers stated that they were in close communication with principals and school leadership teams and did not need regular meeting with coaches. For example, a superintendent said: "I don't need direct contact with service providers. The principal keeps me informed, and I've been in the school when providers are there and know what the school is doing." However, the majority pushed for greater integration of districts in building-level CSR efforts. A district coordinator of school improvement stated:

Overall Middle Start provided a good model, played a critical friend's role and was there to meet the needs of staff. Middle Start is more involved at the school level—the coach's time is theirs [the school's]. But the structure of the model must be tightly knit with districts. The building administration makes requests and asks questions at the district level and I have to then explore the issue because I don't receive the information from Middle Start. There has been a disconnect.

An assistant superintendent stated:

We try to eliminate barriers that only a district can. But CSR coaches are not interfacing with us. Interaction with central office is key as principals are talking with us and asking for things. But central office is not fully in the loop as CSR is focused on the building level.

Three respondents also emphasized the district's important role in hiring and retaining administrators and teachers at the school level and the need for CSR program–district collaboration on minimizing the effects of staff turnover on program implementation and school improvement. They referred to "school readiness" or "school context" as a critical issue influencing the implementation of Middle Start in schools and stated that turnover issues affecting schools and districts often disrupted school improvement.

Align and improve professional development

Three district respondents stated that Middle Start professional development needed to be better aligned with district requirements and initiatives. In one case, a superintendent stated that the school implementing Middle Start also had to pay attention to implementing the district curriculum and participating in a district technology initiative. Another superintendent was concerned that Middle Start providers planned professional development during the school day instead of after school and stated that Middle Start should pay attention to district limitations on teacher release time when scheduling professional development. A coordinator of school improvement pointed out that literacy across the curriculum was a common goal for the district as well as Middle Start, but that the district literacy initiative endorsed a different program from the one recommended by the Middle Start coach. She noted that Middle Start, the school, and the district needed to discuss both options in more detail to promote greater alignment between program-initiated and district-initiated efforts.

Three respondents also expressed a need for better coaching and professional development in special education inclusion. A superintendent stated: "We are just starting to implement inclusion and have a lot to learn in this area." Another superintendent stated: "Middle Start has made the least progress in the area of inclusion. Special education inclusion is a priority goal for this year. There are no programs that specifically address equity issues." One respondent also noted the need for professional development for family engagement, stating: "Parent engagement is an area of weakness."

Implications for Partnerships with Districts

The majority of district respondents in this study emphasized that greater collaboration with Middle Start program staff would help them improve their own capacity to support grant and non-grant schools with comprehensive improvement. They stated that district capacity for meeting the academic and developmental needs of students in the middle grades had improved. They confirmed their commitment to the staffing needs of interdisciplinary teams based on the positive teacher collaboration and improved student–teacher relationships they observed in schools. District respondents expressed high levels of satisfaction with Middle Start professional development and coaching based on their observations and schools' reports, and stated that they would try to sustain professional development for teachers past the grant period, as the instructional improvements taking place in schools attested to the effects of enhanced teacher learning (although they pushed for improved professional development in specific areas). They also stated that their experience with Middle Start led them to believe that partnerships with external programs infused the system with "new blood" and helped schools gain fresh perspectives and ongoing support to spur improvement. Finally, district leaders discussed the influence of comprehensive school reform on district policy, stating that they were encouraged to move away from piecemeal interventions to holistic and long-term approaches.

These are a highly promising set of findings for improving collaboration of CSR programs and districts, given the major topics outlined in the literature. The literature on the districts' role in school improvement emphasizes district involvement in setting academic standards and conducting academic initiatives, assessment, financial and organizational management, ongoing professional development of teachers and administrators, and parent and community engagement (Hoy & Dipaola, 2009; Tushnet & Harris, 2006; MacIver & Balfanz, 1999). Experts identify the district as the largest provider of professional development for teachers and principals (Spillane, 2000), as the key agent responsible for "scaling up" reforms (Spillane, 2006; MacIver & Farley, 2003; Elmore, 1996), and as a core intermediary between state policy and teachers' practice (Spillane & Thomson, 1997). However, not all districts are successful in performing these tasks. Marsh's (2000) review of the research on district–school relations identified several critiques of districts that minimized the importance of their role in school reform. Research cited the bureaucratic and unresponsive nature of districts and their lack of understanding of and commitment to reform as critical reasons that state, federal, and other initiatives bypassed the district and worked directly with schools (pp. 11–12). Marsh also identified studies demonstrating the value added by districts to improving teaching and learning. Some of the factors contributing to effective school–district partnerships were joint teaching and learning initiatives by districts and schools, high levels of district knowledge of reforms undertaken, and experienced district leadership, open to new learning (pp. 11–12).

In this study, the majority of district respondents demonstrated great interest in understanding school-level improvements, learning more about middle-grades reform and CSR, and applying their new knowledge to crafting new district policies and initiatives. Considering critical and supportive views of the district, it is clear that there is great potential for the district to help schools undertake professional development, scale up promising reforms, and serve as interpreters and guides to state and federal guidelines, leaving the school to focus on teaching and learning by minimizing its administrative responsibilities. These functions of districts make them ideal partners for Middle Start schools and program staff in further advancing comprehensive middle-grades educational reform.

REGIONAL INFRASTRUCTURE FOR REFORM

Corbett and Wilson (2007; Corbett, Fancsali, Gopalan, Weinbaum, & Wilson, 2006) have written extensively on the Middle Start Partnership in Michigan in their role as third-party evaluators of its work. They describe the partnership as an organic but self-governing entity, which

> *...represents a unique approach to reforming middle grades education in this country. While it shares with all other reforms a keen interest in promoting better teaching and learning, the initiative's proponents also have acted on the belief that sustainable comprehensive reform requires the collaboration and coordinated activity of key actors from institutions of higher education (IHE), non-profit social and educational service agencies, school districts, and other interested parties. A partnership of representatives of such organizations augments the intellectual and material resources available to those designing, assisting, and implementing reform and increases the capacity of middle grades advocacy efforts in the state. Of course, numerous educational improvement efforts create affiliated groups that give those involved opportunities to discuss and plan their actions, but MMSP sees itself as a governing and advocacy body that can promote the maintenance and sustainability of middle grades reform. In its creation, then, MMSP required reform among the variety of agencies that had interests in middle grades education in addition to those changes sought at the school level. MMSP therefore is a tangible, extra-organizational entity that seeks to act in the best interests of improved middle grades classrooms while operating at multiple layers of the educational system. ...Viewed thematically, however, Middle Start is much more readily grasped because its numerous participants, their lengthy period of surprisingly intense involvement with one another, and their myriad actions all—from the beginning—coalesced around three simple, albeit not always articulated, ideas:*

- *Middle grades schools should serve youth well academically, developmentally, and equitably.*
- *Building schools' capacity to serve students well would require taking action at multiple layers of the educational system with the involvement of multiple partners.*
- *The partners should communicate, coordinate, and collaborate in an ongoing relationship that would allow them to seize on opportunities to further middle grades reform whenever they appeared. (Corbett et al., 2006, pp. 267–268)*

There were several roles that the MMSP played in Michigan, namely: school-based coaching, engaging districts and the State Department of Education, conducting awareness and advocacy activities within the state to raise public knowledge of middle-grades education, improving teacher preparation and professional development in the middle grades, and research and evaluation for formative as well as summative purposes. In this chapter, I restrict myself to the partnership's role in school-based coaching, as the core of Middle Start was school-based work to improve teaching and learning, and coaches led this critical work.

Coaches belonged to one or the other of following four organizations that were key members of the MMSP:

- Michigan Schools in the Middle (MSIM) at Central Michigan University (CMU) serving the central region (henceforth referred to as CMU).
- Middle Vision at Eastern Michigan University (EMU) serving the southeastern region (henceforth referred to as EMU).
- Michigan Coalition of Essential Schools (MCES) serving the southwestern region and Detroit.
- U.P. Center for Educational Development at Northern Michigan University (NMU) serving the Upper Peninsula (henceforth referred to as NMU).

These organizations meet with other members of the partnership on a quarterly basis to further their joint work (e.g., development of a theory of action, formation of a steering committee, and integration of professional development and technical assistance). In this role, they "fit" the vision and mission of the partnership with the context of participating schools (and districts), and define what one coach calls, "the non-negotiables" (i.e., Middle Start's goals and dimensions). One of the main strengths as well as challenges of the Middle Start model is its flexibility in response to the local contexts of schools and districts. School-based coaching entailed an understanding of middle-grades educational philosophy and practices and the field of CSR on the part of the coaches. Coaches worked closely, once or twice a week, with teachers and principals within their schools, and when needed also met with district officials. I worked closely with Middle Start coaches for several years, and draw on extensive documentation that my colleague Patricia Jessup and I did on coaching and school improvement as part of our formative studies of Middle Start. Coaches played the following key roles within Middle Start (Gopalan & Jessup, 2001):

- Initiating and sustaining the right goals and processes for school improvement, in alignment with the Middle Start model and the school's own goals.
- Helping the school develop a school improvement plan closely aligned with the goals and dimensions of Middle Start, the needs of the school, and district requirements and policies.
- Building productive relationships with administrators and staff by understanding the culture of the school after careful observations of classrooms, formal and informal interactions with school staff, and review of school documents.
- Developing a school leadership team, composed of school administrators, teacher leaders, and parents, and ensuring that it had wide support within the school.
- Raising awareness of critical concepts and practices in the middle grades through workshops, presentations, hands-on sessions, and informal conversations with administrators, teachers, and other staff in the school.
- Connecting the school with superior professional development opportunities in varied areas, including curriculum, instruction, assessment, developmental responsiveness, and school organization, and ensuring that the focus of the professional development closely matched the school's improvement plan.
- Keeping a bird's-eye view of the school's progress and identifying gaps and weaknesses in the implementation, for refining implementation.
- Integrating multiple initiatives and district requirements so that Middle Start was not an "add-on" that burdened the school, but a vehicle to bring together different strands of improvement.

Neufeld and Roper (2003) state that coaches are the bridge that link design with implementation and research with practice. A key area of MMSP's effort is the preparation and support of coaches, in order for them to truly act as a bridge that strengthens school improvement. Gopalan, West, Montesano, and Hoelscher (2005) describe the coaching network of the MMSP as follows:

- Coaches typically spend 3–4 days per month in each school, working with school leadership teams and teacher teams.
- Coaches are typically former principals, central office administrators, or veteran teachers with very strong credentials.
- Their role is to help leadership teams develop their capacity in goal-setting, implementation, self-assessment, and ongoing improvement of teaching and learning.
- Coaches work with teacher teams to improve teaching and support students when they face social or emotional problems.
- Coaches participate in, and help plan, monthly seminars for school leadership teams, which take the form of a networking meetings of such teams from different regions.
- In turn, coaches participate in their own professional development through monthly meetings with the MMSPs regional director to enhance their own practices through reflection, exchange, and new learning.

Thus, Middle Start schools are embedded layers of support such as coaching, district support, school networks, and the network of coaches, all within the structure of the MMSP, which oversees the overall direction of the effort and connects it with CSR and middle-grades advancements at the national level.

As stated in the introduction, Middle Start went through a rigorous review to gain entry into the national Catalog of School Reform Models, and became one of only 25 designs that schools could select as their CSR partner. Evaluations of the model judged it successful in improving student achievement on comparative studies (Juvonen et al., 2004; Corbett & Wilson, 2007), and Middle Start teachers and partners received awards for the quality of their work. A document titled "Evidence of Effectiveness," compiled from several evaluations, summarizes Middle Start's record on formal assessments as follows (Middle Start National Center, 2007):

The true measure of any school reform effort is whether it made a difference in teacher practice and student achievement. In the case of Middle Start, research indicates that it has. Over a history spanning more than a decade, Middle Start has steadily improved teacher and student performance, as indicated by better test scores in the gatekeeper subjects of reading and math and increased school capacity to support and sustain innovative reform. Findings of several internal and external evaluations, including quasi-experimental studies, confirm that:

- *Middle Start schools consistently outpaced similar schools and state averages in achievement gains;*
- *Student achievement in Middle Start schools improved significantly in reading, mathematics, science, and social studies;*
- *Middle Start schools reported significant improvements in school climate, teacher collaboration, and student engagement in learning;*
- *Middle Start was shown to promote innovations in teaching and learning that lead to the types of positive changes in student learning and achievement described above.*

In this chapter, I described a systemic, collaborative, publically focused partnership initiated by the WKKF and implemented by the AED. With the advent of the national CSR initiative, AED was able to grow the initiative in partnership with Michigan Department of Education. Thus, the systemic partnership gained policy backing and seemed poised to address improvement of teaching and learning on a large-scale, sustainable basis. Middle Start's focus on teaching and learning in detail as it played out at Owen and also presented districts' views of significant improvement in teaching and learning across several districts. Coaches' preparation and school-level networking provided critical support for teaching and learning and allowing the initiative to scale up without diluting its quality. Middle Start grew from a Foundation-sponsored initiative working with 12 schools to a 100-school network of schools dotting the country. National endorsement and federal funding made it look like it would sustain and grow further. The MMSP's joint efforts and relationships with districts and the State Department of Education in Michigan provided a cohesive framework within which school-based work could continue in the long term. The blow to the system delivered by the stoppage of funds to CSR by the federal government could have brought down the whole structure. Although the MMSP lost ground as a result of the stoppage, its roots in the state and credibility with schools and districts have led to new forms of working with schools on a fee-for-service basis or funded through streams other than CSR. I have not studied this as closely as I did the first 10 years of the initiative, but from follow-up conversations with those still involved in this initiative, I understand that it does continue to sustain in Michigan. The National Middle Start Center in New York has also continued to refine and rework the model, and it has since gained traction in New York City and Washington DC, among other regions.

The Middle Start case illustrates the huge support that the program enjoyed among teachers, administrators, and district officials. Third-party evaluations and reviews deemed the program promising in terms of raising student achievement on standardized state tests in Michigan. Despite the stoppage of the CSR funds, which hampered the scale-up and further refinement of Middle Start in the CSR format, the program illustrates the promise inherent in PPPs between committed, reputed nonprofit organizations, and government/public schools.

Chapter 4 discusses a pilot initiative in the Chennai Corporation schools (district-run schools in Chennai). Also a partnership between reputed nonprofit organizations and the Corporation, the pilot began in a handful of schools and experimented with bringing the Montessori Method into government or public schools. Although not as large in scale as Middle Start, the Montessori project, as I have termed it, showed as much promise and succeeded in deeply engaging teachers and students, winning over parents, and impressing district administrators. Riding on a policy wave, much like Middle Start and CSR, the initiative is poised to spread to all preschools and kindergartens within the Corporation of Chennai.

NOTES

1. According to U.S. State Department of Education criteria.
2. AED was acquired by FHI 360 in 2011. FHI 360's website is www.fhi360. org.
3. See http://middlestart.org/resources/for all research reports.
4. View the National Forum's homepage on http://www.mgforum.org/.
5. Title I is a provision in U.S. federal legislation for improving the academic achievement of disadvantaged children. See http://www.ed.gov/policy/ elsec/leg/esea02/pg1.html.
6. The Catalog of School Reform Models is now archived in the Education Resources Information Center (ERIC) database. www.eric.ed.gov.

7. Free or reduced-price lunch eligibility is restricted to students from lower income families in the United States.

8. This press release is archived at http://middlestart.org/images/files_ resources/CCSI_Press_Release_122205.pdf.

9. Names of people and places have been changed in this section for the sake of confidentiality.

10. Aspects of the school may have changed since the time of my last visit. This report documents the school as it was from 1997 to 2002.

11. Interdisciplinary teaming is discussed in detail below. In short, teaming is an organizational practice in the middle grades that schedules common planning time for teachers within a grade level in order to promote thematic, integrated instruction, and coordinated student support.

12. Core Explore is an innovation that afforded additional learning time for students to help them keep up and advance in their work in a small group format.

13. As mentioned in the introduction, 20 percent of students at Owen were in special education in 2000/01.

4

Montessori in Chennai Corporation Schools

Kindergarten classrooms in Chennai Corporation schools seem a world away from schools with middle grades in Michigan. Sitting on the floor of a Montessori classroom in Chennai, as I watch young children industriously grating carrots, matching word and picture cards, and building the pink tower, I think of the children in rural and urban Michigan schools and the models, scripts, and articles they created. In Chennai, little girls and boys walk purposefully to the shelf, carefully replace work that they have completed, and eagerly select something new to work on. In Michigan, the children were much older; some of them were almost as tall as me. They clearly loved thinking, debating, writing, and working in groups, and displayed their work with great pride and satisfaction. The Montessori teacher sits near the children, observing and gently guiding them when needed. The middle school teacher circulated among the groups, listening, participating, and mediating when the discussions became too vociferous. The little children were disciplined, quiet, and immersed in their work. The older children were loud, excited, but also similarly immersed in their work.

Recently, my older son came home after a full day of school, and two hours of after-school soccer, and remarked that he was not at all tired: "I didn't even notice the day go by. It was so much fun." I've observed both my primary school–age children bent over their homework, intently writing their own math problems, creating a crossword puzzle with homophones, or researching early modes of human communication on the Internet. Children love learning. Unfortunately, and perhaps unintentionally, adults have made schooling tiresome and onerous, and damped this love of learning. The two partnerships in this book have succeeded in bringing the joy of learning back into schools. It is noteworthy that both Middle Start and the Montessori project worked with low-performing public schools, serving mainly children from low-income families, and successfully revitalized teaching and learning in them.

Both projects lack conclusive randomized experiments that demonstrate a causal link between the project and gains in student achievement. However, any longitudinal study (qualitative or quantitative) of the schools at the beginning of their involvement with the projects, and over the course of their improvement efforts, would show greater student engagement in learning and more positive views of school. Teachers and teaching were at the core of both initiatives. Any study of teaching would have captured the depth and variety of professional development for teachers in both projects, and shown greater skill and satisfaction with their work.

I began documenting the Corporation–Montessori project in Chennai in 2005.[1] The classes are heterogeneously grouped: Children vary in age from two-and-a-half to six years. Each classroom has at least one trained Montessori teacher. Each classroom is also assigned a helper who cleans the room and assists with the children. During my weekly visits to the schools, I became familiar with the children and teachers, and documented their journey as they began the Montessori project. The project worked with government-run schools in five Chennai neighborhoods: Mylapore, Kottur, Saidapet, Velachery, and Thondiarpet over the course of my study. I spent most of my time at Kottur and Saidapet, as these had several Montessori environments each.

Additionally, I documented the Montessori teacher education diploma program, in which over 90 Corporation teachers participated on a part-time basis, in order to capture the experiences of teachers as they retrained in this method. I also recorded the perspectives and experiences of Corporation officials, Montessori trainers, and sponsors, as they moved from their first steps in one school toward a coherent plan to refine and expand the program.

Overall, I interviewed about 45 teachers, including those in Montessori classrooms and in the part-time course. I interviewed about 50 parents, including those who dropped off their children in the Corporation schools at Mylapore, Kottur, and Saidapet.[2] I made weekly visits to the schools, focusing mostly on Saidpet and Kottur, and visiting Mylapore and Thondiarpet on a quarterly basis. I conducted formal interviews and had several informal conversations with Padmini Gopalan of Sri Ramacharan Charitable Trust, Uma Shanker of the Center for Montessori Training, Chennai (the two not-for-profit organizations involved in the project), and Nithya Kalyani, the lead teacher, who set up the environments at Mylapore, Kottur, and Saidapet. Given the busy schedules of Corporation officials, I conducted only one interview with the lead officer of the project. Thus, the perspectives of the educational partners are richly represented in this chapter, while Corporation officials may seem to have less of a voice. However, it was with their consent and encouragement that the project began and grew, and I take that as a tacit affirmation of their support for the Montessori work in the Chennai Corporation schools. However, dozens of Corporation teachers and the principals of participating schools added their perspectives throughout the study.

This chapter begins with an overview of research on Montessori education within the context of constructivist theories of preschool education, reports on studies of the effects of Montessori exposure on academic and other outcomes in the long term, and summarizes critiques of the Montessori approach. The chapter goes on to outline the place of Montessori education in the Indian context, before moving on to discussions of teaching and learning within the Montessori project in Chennai.[3]

THE MONTESSORI METHOD

Maria Montessori's emphasis on learning as an innate part of child development and her belief that education elicits and enhances this process set her apart from the thinking of her time. In *The Absorbent Mind*, she wrote (Montessori, 1967):

> *The education of our day is rich in methods, aims, and social ends, but it takes no account of life itself. ... Scholastic machinery is estranged from social life as if this and all its problems were outside its compass. ... The concept of an education centered upon the care of the living being alters all previous ideas. ... What has to be defended is the construction of human normality. Have not all our efforts been aimed at removing obstacles from the child's path of development? ... This is education, understood as a help to life. (pp. 10–17)*

Montessori, in various lectures and writings, referred to a set of innate human tendencies that she had arrived at through extensive observations of small children: exploration, orientation, order, imagination, manipulation, repetition, precision, control of error leading to perfection, and communication. She built her approach to education appealing to these tendencies, as she believed it would help children in their natural path of adaptation to their environment. Research on Montessori education documents the learning experiences of children in Montessori environments from early childhood into elementary school, and demonstrates how they grasp major language and mathematical, social, and scientific concepts through this form of education. Research also emphasizes social factors such as cooperative learning, development of learning communities within multiage environments, and the effects of modes of non-punitive assessment and review on learners' confidence and eagerness to learn (Lillard, 1996).

Montessori is often cited along with Piaget, Dewey, and Bruner as a leading constructivist (Mooney, 2005; Lillard, 1996). Constructivism is founded on the premise that the child actively develops knowledge through engagement in meaningful activities, as he or she interacts with peers and guides, and progressively expands upon frames of understanding and experience (Piaget, 1967). This contradicts a traditional/behaviorist view that the child is a receiver of knowledge, a blank slate, on which the teacher and school can write objective information (Thorndike, 1962).[4] According to Lillard (2005), Montessori was the only leading constructivist to leave behind a "broad, detailed curriculum. Dewey had many ideas that withstood the test of time, but he did not leave the legacy of a full curriculum," she states (p.13).

Lillard additionally credits Montessori with several insights about child development and learning that were borne out by later theoretical discoveries:

She drew extensively on the idea of sensitive periods. ...Among other sensitive periods, Dr. Montessori identified the first five years as a sensitive period for language in children. She went so far as to claim the innateness of human language years before Noam Chomsky (1959) rocked the world of psycholinguistics with the same claim. She talked repeatedly of how important early experience is to development, well before research in neuroscience backed the idea. ...In these and other ways, Dr. Montessori was clearly well ahead of her time. (pp. 33–34)

While Montessori education has carved a niche in the world of early childhood and elementary education, many raise questions regarding its contribution to long-term academic development and performance.

There are few "scientific" studies of the longitudinal effects of Montessori education on academic indicators in high school and beyond. Two comparative studies, discussed later, show that Montessori education is significant in enhancing students' performance on standardized math and science tests in high school. Montessori students fared much better than students from traditional pre- and elementary schools. Also students' self-rankings on surveys of psychosocial indicators, preparation for the future, career readiness, and social relationships showed that students with higher levels of Montessori exposure in the early years expressed greater confidence and independence compared to a peer sample that attended non-Montessori schools. Lillard's (2005) work is one of few systematic attempts to evaluate Montessori education by looking at its core principles and activities in light of related research. Lillard concludes that Montessori was ahead of her times in her insights regarding child development and learning. She writes: "Montessori education, then, seems more in line than traditional schooling is with what we know about children's development, how they learn, and the conditions under which they thrive" (p. 328).

A randomized study by Lillard and Else-Quest (2006)set up an experiment in which students assigned to Montessori or other public schools by a computerized lottery were studied as "treatment" and "matched control" groups respectively. Students were given a set of academic/cognitive and social-behavioral tests in two age cohorts. According to the authors: "Overall, 53 control and 59 Montessori students were studied (table S1). The 5-year-old group included 25 control and 30 Montessori children, and the 12-year-old group included 28 control and 29 Montessori children" (p. 1893). Students were matched mainly on parental income. The researchers found that students from the Montessori sample demonstrated better social and academic skills relative to the control group. They write:

> *On several dimensions, children at a public inner city Montessori school had superior outcomes relative to a sample of Montessori applicants who, because of a random lottery, attended other schools. By the end of kindergarten, the Montessori children performed better on standardized tests of reading and math, engaged in more positive interaction on the playground, and showed more advanced social cognition and executive control. They also showed more concern for fairness and justice. At the end of elementary school, Montessori children wrote more creative essays*

with more complex sentence structures, selected more positive responses to social dilemmas, and reported feeling more of a sense of community at their school. (p. 1894)

Studies by Dohrmann (2003) and her associates (Dohrmann, Nishida, Gartner, Lipsky, & Grimm, 2007) in Milwaukee also found superior math and science performance in high school by students who attended Montessori schools at the elementary level, as compared to their classmates who attended regular elementary schools within the same system. Dohrmann writes (2003):

In essence, attending a Montessori program from the approximate ages of three to eleven predicts significantly higher mathematics and science standardized test scores in high school. ... It was found five to seven years after the students had exited the Montessori programs and enrolled in traditional public schools. (p. 3)

In an electronic supplement to their 2006 article, Lillard and Else-Quest (2006) also summarize other studies of Montessori programs, showing that

students attending Montessori middle schools, relative to matched controls, were significantly more likely to report 1) feeling energized and engaged while doing schoolwork; 2) spending more time doing schoolwork and less time socializing and watching media during school; 3) that their friends and classmates are one and the same people; and 4) that their classrooms are orderly, that their teachers are supportive, and that they feel emotionally safe at school.

They also cited research on Head Start programs, finding that infants who were randomly assigned to a Montessori Head Start program had "superior language and cognitive skills relative to other infants at 4 time points from 14 to 36 months of age." Looking across the spectrum of school reform movements, Lillard and Quest also cite a meta-analysis of 29 school reforms by Borman, Hewes, Overman, and Brown (2003), which found that: "Montessori obtained one of the largest effects on achievement (d = .27) despite the Montessori schools averaging only 3 years of implementation."

Holfester (2008), in an overview essay on Montessori, however reports that some studies have found little evidence of higher academic achievement in Montessori schools. He writes:

> *A recent expansive review of Montessori and traditional programs in New York schools failed to support the hypothesis that enroll- ment in a Montessori school was associated with higher academic achievement (Lopata, Wallace, & Finn, 2005). Miller and Bizzell's (1984) long-term study of pre-school education and high school curricula in 1984 also found no difference between Montessori and traditional instruction.*

This 100-year old system has its share of critics. Some equate Montessori education with the method, as it requires a highly controlled environment and particular skills on the part of the teacher. The rigid sequence and structure of Montessori schools, and their unchanging norms, despite a century of practice, are often critiqued. Additionally, some criticize the method for casting children in the role of workers within a strict structure, as it prematurely enforces adult norms on children. For example, Polakow (cited in Holfester, 2008) writes: "The (Montessori) school imposed an adult-defined work ethic on children, socialized children to engage in work in isolation from others, and produced a work ethic where productivity, efficiency and conformity are perceived as synonymous with healthy development" (p. 4).

A volley of criticism came in the 1960s from progressive educators, following John Dewey's thinking, who stated that the highly controlled Montessori environment did not allow children to experience discovery on their terms. They even equated the approach's perceived rigidity with that of traditional schooling. Smith (2005) lists the following critiques of the Montessori Method by influential progressive educators:

1. Inadequate time for social cooperation and interactive play.
2. Materials were limited in their range of uses.
3. Low emphasis on creativity and imagination.
4. Unnecessary emphasis on the training of the senses.
5. Overemphasis on work as a preparation for further ends.
6. No direct relationship to the real world.
7. Overreliance on mechanical manipulation of materials with little time for free play.
8. Overly individualistic; high emphasis on auto-education and self-correcting materials.

Thus, like most institutions and systems, Montessori has its share of supporters and critics. Lillard (2005) states that the elementary materials developed by Mario Montessori, Maria Montessori's son (some of which were developed in India), showed a greater emphasis on social interaction and experiential learning, perhaps in response to the critiques of progressive educators.

MONTESSORI IN INDIA

Maria Montessori and her son, Mario Montessori, spent several years in India during the World War II years. They were interned within India, in Chennai and Tamil Nadu, for almost nine years over two visits. The elementary Montessori program was developed in Tamil Nadu, and piloted in Kodaikanal (a town in the hills of Tamil Nadu) by Mario Montessori before he left India in the mid-1940s. During this time, Maria Montessori also conducted teacher preparation programs at the Theosophical Society and Kalakshetra, both reputed institutions of learning and culture in Chennai (Indian Montessori Foundation, n.d.). Educators who trained with her began to spread the message of Montessori education, and it found roots in several Indian cities in the following decades. At least three recognized bodies provide teacher preparation and accreditation programs in India: the Indian Montessori Center (IMC) in Bangalore with chapters in Karnataka and Tamil Nadu; the Association Montessori Internationale (AMI), with branches in Chennai, Hyderabad, and Mumbai; and the Indian Montessori Association (IMA) in Bangalore.

A defining factor in setting up Montessori schools is the significant capital cost, as the finely graded sequence of Montessori activities in each area of learning, as well as the high-quality wood and finish of the materials increase their cost. Each classroom requires a dedicated set of materials, multiplying the cost on a school-wide basis. Montessori schools have traditionally only been available to the middle and upper classes in urban centers of India. At the Congress held to celebrate the centenary of Maria Montessori in Bangalore in 2007, Indian Montessorians discussed the urgent need to take this child-centric system of education to less-privileged groups. [5]

There are movements in several parts of the world to bring promising educational innovations within the reach of disadvantaged groups through partnerships with public systems. In India, Digantar in Rajasthan and Eklavya in Madhya Pradesh, for example, work with government bodies in these states to improve curriculum and instruction through long-term partnerships. The Chennai Montessori project is another such effort, and the rest of this chapter details the partnership between the Corporation of Chennai and two private nonprofit trusts as they work toward the goal of bringing an excellent preschool education to the children attending government schools in Chennai.

THE CHENNAI PROJECT

An informal arrangement between Sri Ramacharan Charitable Trust (SRCT), a charitable organization with an interest in education for the underprivileged, and a Corporation school in Mylapore is the starting point for the initiative. Padmini Gopalan, the president of SRCT, said that she initially set up the Trust with small contributions of money from her family and friends to aid Corporation schools in helping struggling students stay in school and progress in their education. Padmini was concerned about the high rate of drop out at the elementary level, and the implication it had for the future prospects of students from indigent families. She approached the principal of a school near her home in Mylapore to see what needs the school had, and whether SRCT could help in some way.

Padmini said:

We did not have a clear plan at first. We just wanted to help, and when so the first thing we did was offer free tuitions to students who were behind in their work. We used to visit the school and conduct English classes, tuitions, and special activities at assigned times.

Soon SRCT raised enough funds from donors, including Child Vikaas International—a Los Angeles–based funding organization, to place a full-time teacher at the school to substitute for absent teachers, and continue offering classes and tuitions. However, trustees began to question if this was the best course of action and began brainstorming other ways of helping the school. Padmini said: "We wanted to go to someone who knew a lot about education and see what they said. So we contacted Uma (Shanker) and that is how this all started."

Uma Shanker, the director of the Center for Montessori Training–Chennai (CMT-C), now a part of Kalvi Trust for Research and Education (Kalvi), was primarily involved in teacher preparation in the Montessori Method. CMT-C is a well-known name in education circles in Chennai, as several of their alumni work in Montessori schools in and around Chennai and a few have established their own schools. Uma and Chitra Mani, the associate director of CMT-C, were also involved in preparing teachers in Nagapattinam and Erode, as they wanted their work to have a rural base. They were involved in a few NGO-run educational projects, as they are passionate about high-quality early childhood education for disadvantaged children. They were excited about working with the Mylapore school and suggested that SRCT consider setting up Montessori environments in the school, and that they would help find a teacher and set up the classrooms. Uma said: "We strongly felt that Montessori is not just for the privileged few. We really welcomed the chance to work in the Corporation schools with Sri Ramacharan Charitable Trust."

The project began to take shape as SRCT and CMT-C got permission from the Corporation to begin a Montessori classroom within the Mylapore school. Forces within the Corporation created a favorable environment for the Trusts to pilot the first Montessori environments. With the advent of SSA (Education for all, the policy initiative that brought ABL to Tamil Nadu, discussed in Chapter 2), forward-thinking officials had begun to seek expert partners to update and upgrade the public delivery of education. M. P. Vijayakumar, a veteran IAS[6] officer, and State Director for SSA, Tamil Nadu, is quoted in an interview, saying (Srinivasan, 2008):

How do children learn? Children automatically pick up their mother tongue. Many learn to operate gadgets such as the television remote, cell phone, and instantly pick up songs. If they can learn so many things outside the classroom, what prevents them from learning inside the class? Branding the child as intelligent or not intelligent is not right. It is really the system's failure.

A study commissioned by the Corporation of Chennai on classroom practices and reasons behind the low achievement of children in Corporation schools found that direct instruction and rote learning were two of the reasons behind low achievement and dropout in the system. The report noted that teacher-directed approaches, the lecture method, and rote learning were predominant in the schools in the study; students were seen as receivers of knowledge; teachers assumed that all students could learn at the same pace and perform equally; students did not have opportunities for experiential and ABL; evaluation was traditional; and there was little scope for student initiative because of instructional and time constraints (Sarva Shikhsha Abhiyan, n.d.).

The report recommended the implementation of ABL throughout the system to promote group- and self-directed learning, thoughtful and well-presented materials for learning, freedom to select activities based on students' interest, learning at students' own pace, integrated evaluation, positive student–teacher interaction, and all-round development of the child (Sarva Shiksha Abhiyan, n.d.).

Rishi Valley' Education Center's curriculum,[7] adapted as the system-wide ABL program, was already being implemented in the primary grades in many government schools within Tamil Nadu, and is touted as a working model that can be refined and replicated throughout the country.[8] Corporation officials were open to the idea of testing Montessori education in the kindergarten sections of one or two schools. However, they were not able to bear the costs of the sets of material required for each classroom, which ran into several thousands each.

SRCT raised funds for Montessori materials from Child Vikaas International, a major donor based in Los Angeles, even as CMT-C canvassed their students to see who of the graduating class would like to work in the Mylapore school. Padmini laughs as she remembers looking at the list of materials presented to her by CMT-C, and the cost attached to them. She said:

I was shocked to see what they would cost. I wondered if it was worth it. But after all my talks with CMT-C, and my growing understanding of the Montessori system, I felt we had to try it out. I felt the children deserved something good.

Nithya Kalyani, a student from the CMT-C course, joined SRCT's pilot project at Mylapore. Nithya felt that the newness of the idea was both exciting and challenging, and was eager to be a part of the project.

Thus, from offering tuitions and placing a special teacher in the school, the project developed into a concerted effort to improve teaching and learning at the kindergarten level. Slowly, the program grew into a kindergarten-wide Montessori program and has been fully integrated into the Mylapore school over a period of 8 years.

The parents at the Mylapore school work as laborers and domestic helpers and live in the working-class neighborhood surrounding the school. I am unsure if parents are fully aware of the details of the Montessori approach, but in interviews the majority of them reported being very impressed by it as they see the children highly engaged in their school life, and it gave them hope that their child would continue their schooling and find good jobs later. The following are some parent perspectives:

"I did not like this at first. I thought the children would not learn anything and would play all day with the things in the class. They did not get homework, and did not write anything. But slowly I saw how my son stopped crying to go to school and instead cried if he had to be absent! How he was so interested in the things in the classroom."

"My son is so eager to go to school. He hates to miss even one day. He does not shout and make trouble like he used to. Instead he tells me how to behave! He has learned a lot of names of vegetables, fruits, and is curious about everything. He knows English words. It is like sending him to a private school!"

"The teacher never complains now about my child. All the time what I used to hear were complaints and complaints. They don't shout at the children. Somehow the children just seem to like it here and the teacher doesn't need to shout. This is a big surprise!"

"This school is helping me realize my dreams for my child. My life has been one of only hardship. I can now hope that he will get a good education and escape these difficulties!"

Each classroom has a Montessori-trained teacher. Corporation teachers at Mylapore were initially resistant about allowing a different approach to be used in their classrooms, and for someone from another organization to be present in their classroom with them. According to Nithya, the resistance went away for many teachers when they saw the interest with which the children worked. Teachers' perspectives are discussed in greater detail in a following section of this chapter. Children's engagement with the materials and their overall experiences are also discussed in a coming section. For parents and teachers at the Mylapore school, it seems that there is no going back to the old way of doing things. The positive experiences of students, parents, and teachers within this school spurred the Trust, CMT-C, and the Corporation to expand the program to other schools.

The second school to participate in the project was located in Kottur, and served a neighborhood similar to the one in Mylapore. Things did not go well in this school due to the principal and teachers' resistance to change their existing approach. The principal stated once that she felt people were "walking in and asking us to do things their way! We have our own way of doing things, which have worked for a long time. Let them go somewhere else with this program." Despite a 6-month engagement with the school, SRCT, CMT-C, and the teachers were unable to convince the principal to allow them to continue their work there. Corporation officials tried to intervene and persuade the school authorities to continue the work, but after months of trying, all sides decided to end the work at Kottur, and select a new school. The project ran from August 2006 to February 2007 at this school, and despite requests from parents to continue with the Montessori environments, the project was discontinued.

A Corporation school at Saidapet was the new choice. Nithya, who had handed over her Mylapore classroom to another CMT-C-trained teacher, and moved on to Kottur, was given the charge to set up seven new classroom environments at Saidpet. Observing the skill with which she set about preparing the Saidapet environments led me to believe that the project was building her leadership skills, as much as it was honing her teaching. Six new graduates of the CMT-C course joined the Saidapet school in June 2007. The inauguration, attended by representatives of the Corporation, the Trusts, and school was a festive affair. It was clear that a lot was riding on the fate of the Montessori project at the Saidapet school. The large number of rooms; the heightened level of organization and partnership between the Corporation, SRCT, and CMT-C; and the warm welcome the project received from the principal of the school ensured that it began on a strong note. I observed the program for the first year on an almost weekly basis, and found that despite occasional issues between Corporation teachers and Montessori teachers all seven classrooms settled into their routines quickly, and continued to develop well. Parent responses mirrored what I heard in Mylapore, and parents, though confused about the details of Montessori education, felt that overall children loved going to school and were spending their time there well.

SRCT initially raised the funds needed for Mylapore and Saidapet from private donors. However, after the successful and relatively smooth establishment of seven environments at Saidapet, Corporation officials, SRCT, and CMT-C were convinced that this had to be taken system-wide. What Saidapet offered was a larger canvas within which they could view the ease with which children adapted to the system, and whether there was parental support for it. Mylapore, the older of the two pilot schools, showed that children who spent three years in a Montessori environment effortlessly transitioned into a regular first grade class-room, and had the requisite math, language, and other skills required to learn and thrive in a non-Montessori classroom. First grade teachers at Saidapet and Mylapore noticed and remarked on the enhanced capacities of the first groups of Montessori preschoolers entering first grade. While I have interviewed first grade teachers, this aspect needs more study and warrants a wider as well as closer look at first grade classrooms.

While Mylapore was where the first steps took place, Saidapet was where the project began to scale up. I remember Nithya, the lead teacher, worrying about managing seven new environments at Saidpet. However, the school, with the active help of the principal, Corporation supervisors, and Trust staff smoothly moved into top gear in a few months. I describe classrooms at the Saidapet school in a later section of this chapter.

The Corporation school at Thondiarpet, which joined the project in June 2008, to me, is the third point in this unfolding partnership. It also seems to represent a significant turning point in the implementation as it has great implications for scaling up the initiative and institutionalizing good practices from the pilot. Also, the Corporation has lifted the burden of fundraising for materials and teacher certification from the Trusts and borne the expenses of the Thondiarpet effort. In addition, dozens of Corporation teachers are being trained through the part-time Montessori diploma course at CMT-C. The costs of teacher participation in the course are being borne by the Corporation, in an act of overt support to the program. I interviewed a representative of the Education Department at the Corporation of Chennai, and was struck with his familiarity and enthusiasm for the Montessori Method. The officer, who requested he remain unnamed, said:

> *This is definitely something that we want to see continue. The children are clearly learning, and the teachers too are learning! We see a lot of support from teachers and parents, and we can see why. Children do not need reminding or shouting. They want to pick up the material and figure it out.*

He raised the issue of cost, saying: "It is a one-time cost, but it is very high if we have to supply all classrooms with the materials." When I asked about the future of the project in Chennai, he said: "We would like to support it, but I cannot talk too much about this now." When I asked if he had any reservations or saw any challenges, he said: "None at all. This is a very good method, and we are able to see children learning better."

LEARNING

The following sections provide snapshots of Montessori classrooms I observed at Mylapore, Saidpet, and Thondiarpet, and describe the teacher certification program for Corporation teachers at CMT-C. The Saidapet and Mylapore schools are both located in congested, working-class neighborhoods. As is typical of Corporation schools, their grounds, in contrast to their surroundings, are spacious and green.

Usually the day starts with a few minutes of silent prayer. On several visits, the first activity of the day is a group language activity. Today, children are learning the sound "in" (phonetic usage for the letter "N") and connecting it to vocabulary words such as "nest," "nose," and "newspaper." The children are mostly Tamil speakers. English is a second language that they acquire mainly in school. The children sit around the oval. Some are restless, some still, as they wait for the teacher to set up the activity. One child spreads a large mat. Another brings the language cards, each with a picture of an object starting with "N." The teacher sits on the mat and draws out a card. She places it on the mat and labels the object. She says: "Nose." Children repeat the word. They similarly go through the entire set of cards, emphasizing the first sound as they pronounce the words.

This activity continues for about 15 minutes, after which they go to the mat box and take a mat in an orderly fashion. They begin independent work, choosing activities from an array of Exercises of Practical Life (EPL) and preliminary activities, sensorial, language, and math activities. The following are examples of the types of activities seen over the last six months in the three environments:

- EPL includes activities that are routinely seen in the home, such as rolling rotis, grinding pulses, applying face powder and *bindi*, cutting carrots, sieving, and pouring.[9]

- Preliminary activities include doing puzzles, sorting shapes, building with blocks, threading beads, and looking at board books.
- Sensorial activities include cylinder blocks, the pink tower, brown stairs, texture boards, and color tablets.
- Language activities include a variety of themed cards (e.g., fruits), sound cards (e.g., representing words beginning with a single sound), and paired cards (e.g., animals and their young), letters made of sandpaper, a moveable alphabet for building works, among other activities.
- Mathematical activities include number rods, spindle boxes, cards and counters, and golden bead material.

Montessori teachers and Corporation teachers usually divided the day into time for Montessori activities (mat work and group work), and regular activities of learning alphabets, numbers, and concepts from texts using direct learning. I observed several times that Montessori teachers would use the first half of the morning from about 9 to 11 am for their activities, and Corporation teachers would do reading and writing activities from 11 am to 12:00 pm. This system evolved from discussions between Montessori and Corporation teachers, as the latter were concerned that they would not have an active teaching role, and would not be able to cover the curriculum they were assigned to teach.

In about half the environments this arrangement resulted in a smooth transition from Montessori activities to rote activities. In about half the classrooms, it caused stress between the teachers as they did not support each other, and instead waited for "her part" to finish before "my part begins." Some Corporation teachers, from the beginning, appreciated the Montessori approach and tried to learn the method through observation and coaching from their co-teachers. Others resisted learning the new approach, as they felt they were doing what they were assigned to do as kindergarten teachers, and it was what parents and authorities wanted them to do. Here are two perspectives from teachers, pro and con:

I never raise my voice. I don't use the ruler to make children listen. The children find the material very interesting and they work with it silently. I don't have to shout to teach them. I have learned how to explain things to children, and to let them figure things out instead of constantly correcting them. I love this method.

It may be a good method, but we have to change everything
even if we don't want to.

I noticed the many shoe racks that line the corridor of the Montessori section of the Saidapet school, with children's footwear of varying colors and sizes arranged neatly in them. There are seven Montessori classrooms at this school, with nearly identical organizational arrangements. Montessori equipment, including EPL, sensorial, mathematical, and language activities, are arranged neatly on painted shelves along the walls. The children are grouped in multiage cohorts, in which the smallest children work on puzzles and sorting activities, while the older children work on a range of sensorial, mathematical, and language activities.[10]

A boy, probably aged around five years, walks back and forth from the shelves to his mat, bringing rods of different lengths. He then sits down and concentrates on arranging the rods in sequence. Finally he brings a small box with number cards and arranges numbers from 1 through 10 next to the rods. When done, he calls softly to the teacher to come and see his work. She sits next to him and they go over the arrangement, after which he takes each rod back with the same care to its place on the shelf.

The children work on in a comfortable silence, selecting work from the shelves, figuring it out by themselves on the mats, and putting it back when they are done. In some instances the teacher works with the children, giving them analytical activities to build on their knowledge. For example, a child is working on an activity called the "brown stairs," and once it is complete the teacher shows her how to combine it with the pink tower to conduct a more complex activity that relates size, ratio, and proportion. A boy on the next mat is trying to figure out the binomial cube, which he finds extremely puzzling. What I am intrigued by is his perseverance, as he keeps taking out pieces and putting them back in an order that he hopes will emerge. The girl on the mat next to him is matching pictures with words. She sounds out each letter on the word card phonetically, trying to reach the word through the sounds. The words are written in Tamil, the mother tongue of most of the children. The children are engaged with a range of activities. What is common to them is their interest in their work.

A striking feature of this project is the low incidence of arguments and fights among students. There were a few incidents of children grouping to talk, but often it was to ask for help with an activity or watch a child learn a new activity. A few children got distracted during their work and wandered off to do something else, but eventually did come back and put away the work, without completing it. There were very few instances of children crying or refusing to do work. Most of the time there was near silence in the classroom, and children worked independently on their mats without event. Teachers, especially those with a Montessori background, did not say much to the children, either by way of encouragement or reprimand. For instance, a teacher asked a boy who was walking around to sit down and find something interesting to do. Another teacher told a girl who had done her math problems accurately that she got it all right. There was an economy of speech during the time children worked on their mats. Many Corporation teachers remarked on this as the greatest difference between their prior ways of teaching and the Montessori approach. A teacher said: "We used to shout and shout to get their attention. We used to raise the stick to make them listen. That is not necessary now. They want to use the materials and do it mostly by themselves. Our role has become very different." In one classroom I noticed a Montessori teacher picking up a stick, previously used to scare students, to point out something on a chart displayed high on the wall.

In a few instances, I also observed new students, usually between 2.5 and 3 years of age, quickly adapting to their lives as kindergarten students, as they were eager to roll out a mat and pick materials that attracted them. For instance, a girl clung to her mother crying for some time, but slowly left her side to explore the shelves of puzzles, pouring equipment, blocks, and other objects. She picked up the blocks, the teacher helped her unroll a mat, and with the teacher quietly sitting at her side, the girl began threading the large beads on a string, as her mother left, unnoticed. In another classroom, a little boy initially refused to leave his mother's side, but could not help watching an older child who was solving a puzzle. The colorful puzzles, blocks, utensils for grating, rolling dough, and sifting beans, and other early activities are of great interest to small children, and quickly help them adapt to their new lives as preschoolers.

The next few years will determine whether the project will fulfill its promise and reach all schools in the Corporation of Chennai. So far, it has been characterized by high levels of commitment from SRCT, CMT-C, and the Corporation to growing the project one school at a time. Montessori-trained teachers have worked hard to build bridges with Corporation teachers and share time, space, and routines as new and old approaches coexist in the same classroom. This last year has seen the project begin to win Corporation teachers over from their prior knowl-edge and practices to the Montessori approach. With the Corporation pledging resources and time teacher workshops and materials, the project is poised to scale-up in the coming years. In this section, I sum-marize the major patterns that I recorded across the environments. In the following section I discuss the perspectives of Corporation teachers who are retraining to become Montessori teachers. The chapter concludes with an analysis of the partnership underlying the Chennai project, and what it says about public–private partnerships that seek to improve education.

Some reflections on teaching and learning as they manifested in Montessori environments in Saidpet, Mylapore, and Velachery:

Children's *love of order* was apparent as the project unfolded. For example, children described by Corporation teachers as "noisy," "rowdy," and "unused to discipline," became composed and focused. Even as early as a month into the project, a noisy gaggle of children entered their classroom after their snack break. They ran and walked around the oval painted on the floor, before forming a straggly line to pick up their mats. They quietly found a spot, laid down the mat, and went to choose an item of work. In less than five minutes, the post-break rush had settled into a comfortable silence, each child immersed in his or her own work. This routine continued through each visit, even as the work presented by teachers became more advanced.

The children's *love of activity* was also obvious over the period of documentation, as they engaged in individual and group activities with eager curiosity. During the first class, children beaded, threaded flowers, grated carrots, rolled rotis, sorted shapes, built with blocks, and solved simple puzzles. As the months progressed, children began learning letter sounds and vocabulary and engaging in sensorial activities that devel-oped their understanding of depth, height, volume, shape, order, and the relation of one object to another within an activity. As students advanced they began learning Arithmetic and develop their reading skills, again through varied Montessori activities. Through each phase, children have demonstrated a need to perfect each activity through trial and error, and repetition, as they work on each piece of material several times, until their curiosity is satisfied, and they are ready to move on to something new.

Children's *ability to monitor their own behavior* was also apparent as they became familiar with the routine over the months. In one room, for example, after two months, children knew that they did a short prayer sitting in an oval. So they learned to sit in an oval formation as soon as they walked into the room in the morning. They knew that language activities were next. So they continued to sit in the oval, as the Montessori teacher prepared the activity and sat down on the demonstration mat with them. After circle time, they went to get their mats in an orderly fashion, neatly lay down the mats in rows, chose material from the shelves, and settled down to work on their material. A half-hour before lunch, the Corporation teacher convened them for storytelling or oral reading of alphabets and numbers from the Corporation-assigned texts. Children transitioned from community to individual and back to community activities with ease. As the months progressed, most children went from one activity to the next without prompts or scolding.

The *teacher as a guide-on-the-side* can be very effective, rather than in the traditional role as director and controller of curriculum and instruction. For example, Montessori teachers spent some time each day demonstrating a new activity to individual children, to a small group, or to the entire group. But for most of the time, they silently watched the class, sometimes seated, sometimes slowly circling the room. They rarely corrected or directed. They rarely encouraged or praised. If a child asked for help, they went up to her, but only to urge her to try again and figure it out by herself. I saw several children take apart their work and try to redo it till they got it right, without the teacher prompting them to do so.

TEACHING

In 2008, the project expanded to include Corporation schools at Velachery and Thondiarpet. The format at Velachery was similar to that of Saidpet and Mylapore, in that Montessori-trained teachers from CMT-C and Corporation teachers worked as pairs in each classroom. The Thondiarpet example is very different that the teachers are all Corporation teachers participating in CMT-C part-time certification course to become Montessori teachers, and represents what the project could look like if this PPP sustains in the long term.

Thondiarpet is reminiscent of the pace and feel of the Madras of the past. The Corporation school at Thondiarpet is in a small, quiet lane off a windy road along the beach. The neighborhood is a mix of fisher-folk settlements and working-class homes. The school has a large central courtyard and the primary grades with four Montessori classrooms occupy part of the ground floor of the sprawling building.

I enter the first room, where a teacher is demonstrating new work to a small group of children. After she completes the demonstration, children select work from the shelves and begin working independently on their mats. The teacher divides her time between helping children learn new material and observing the children as they work. She attended the part-time Montessori program offered by CMT-C to Corporation teachers, as part of the collaboration between CMT-C and the Corporation of Chennai, which she completed in summer 2008, along with three other teachers from her school. She was part of the first batch of six teachers to participate in this program, which was piloted in 2007–2008 and lasted a year.[11]

The second batch of teachers participated in the CMT-C course in late 2008 and will conclude in October 2009. This batch has 69 teachers who attend classes three times a week, at CMT-C. Teachers from schools similar to the Thondiarpet Corporation school participated in the Montessori course, which enables them to competently use this method. Initially teachers opposed this decision vehemently with protests and meetings in which they asked the Corporation to withdraw the order requiring them to retrain. However, those that took the course have become advocates for Montessori education, and there is great enthusiasm at several schools, including Thondiarpet, for this change.

The teachers at Thondiarpet are clearly excited about the program. One teacher says:

I feel like I have a new perspective. It is refreshing because I don't think of children the same way, of teaching the same way. I feel ready to do something new, not scared or hesitant. I thought it would be hard to work and train at the same time, but it was worth it! This is a complete method—we are ready to take it forward.

It was during this first visit to Thondiarpet that I had the overwhelming feeling that I was witnessing something revolutionary. By this time I had visited several Montessori classrooms in Corporation schools. I had been to the same classrooms several times to document them over the months for my ethnographic study. However, my excitement came from the fact that these were class acts conducted by Corporation teachers themselves, and not Montessori teachers from outside the system. In Saidapet, Mylapore, and other places, the teachers were inspired

Montessorians who wanted to work with children from less-privileged backgrounds. They had chosen these schools over the more comfortable experiences they might have had in private schools for middle-class children. Their classrooms were equipped with finely crafted, wooden Montessori materials bought with funds raised by the Trusts. However, in Thondiarpet, original Corporation teachers, used to regular ways of teaching and discipline, were now inspired to teach the Montessori way. The quality of the learning in these classrooms, and the enormous role they play in effecting this learning are clear to them.

Visits to CMT-C intensified the feeling that there is a huge change on the way. Teachers participating in the part-time program had between 5 and 15 years of experience, and had taught in Corporations schools for most of their careers, using the texts and methods prevalent in this context. For them to move away from direct instruction to a guided teaching approach, after years of experience in the former, meant adopting a new belief system regarding teaching and learning. During a visit to the teacher preparation program, I witnessed Corporation teachers learning numeric progression in the Montessori way, and reassessing their understanding of something they already knew and had taught students many times over. The Montessori trainer had illustrated the board with a repeating pattern of a dot, a line, a square, and a cube representing geometric progression, and asked Corporation teachers to calculate 10, 10 × 10, 10 × 10 ×10 and so on to see the repeating shapes. It was clearly an "aha" moment for many, as they saw the shapes reappear in greater and greater magnitudes on the board.

The graduation ceremony where Corporation teachers were awarded their Montessori certificate took place at the Ripon Building, the seat of the Corporation of Chennai. A report on the website of the Indian Montessori Center (2012) describes a festive ceremony, attended by the Mayor, Joint Commissioner of Education, the Education Councilor, and other dignitaries (Indian Montessori Center, 2012). The report states: "The valedictory function for the 20th batch of Centre for Montessori Training-Chennai (CMT-C) consisting of 29 of the teachers of the Corporation of Chennai (COC). ...CMT-C has conducted the course entirely in Tamil for the teachers of the Chennai Schools."

Another report in *The Hindu* (2009) noted that 61 teachers from 10 Corporation zones had graduated from the CMT-C Montessori certification program and were ready to go back to their classrooms and use the method. CMT-C prepared the course in Tamil, the native tongue of most of the teachers, and arranged the schedule so that they were able to balance their teaching with participation in the certification program. Below are excerpts from the report (*The Hindu*, 2009):

> *Sixty-one kindergarten teachers of Corporation schools have armed themselves with a new degree—Diploma in Montessori Education. ... At an event here on Monday, Mayor M. Subramanian gave away certificates to the teachers from the 10 Corporation zones. ... It was a joyous occasion for everyone in the auditorium. ... For the teachers, all with seven to 12 years of experience, it was an achievement as they juggled school and attended this course for around 11 months to develop new skills, knowledge and attitude towards the teaching process. For the team from the Centre for Montessori Training, a unit of Kalvi Trust for Research and Education, it was the first time they prepared Montessori content in Tamil.*

Ninety-six teachers in the preschool and Kindergarten sections of Chennai Corporation schools have participated in CMT-C's Montessori certification program from 2007 through 2012, according to a report from the Indian Montessori Center (2012). In interviews, teachers unanimously dwelled on themes such as feelings of greater competence, a sense of discovery and renewal, a greater understanding of the child, and greater respect for their capacity to learn. Teachers' passion for their learning, and inspiration to do things better were overwhelming. It was hard for me to keep an objective stance in the face of their brimming enthusiasm for renewing their classrooms.

A teacher said:

> *I feel like I have another life to live. One with more meaning. I went through the motions as a teacher so far. I was competent because I have done it for so long. But now my own clarity stuns me. I understand and therefore can teach clearly. The materials will help me and my students explore concepts in depth. This method believes in perfecting knowledge, and that has made me want to improve myself.*

Another teacher said: "I hope we can keep this (Montessori) system in our schools and it doesn't come and go like other programs. We will fight to keep it because our eyes are open now."

Yet another teacher said: "I feel like taking a flag and marching through the city to rouse teachers into a movement for this kind of teaching! I can never go back to what I was doing. What we have gone through in this room is going to change us forever as teachers."

Some teachers stated that they were more aware of what children are capable of learning, and would approach them differently from before as a result. Another teacher said:

> The materials can lead the child to understanding. The child can think and research something on his own. We do not have to stand there and tell them what to do all the time. We have to stand back and let them guess, try, and use their reasoning. This is the biggest difference.

"Children can understand something that is taught in a clear and interesting way. I felt like I was a child as I learned things (in the course) in a different way and understood them much better than before. So a child can do the same," a teacher stated.

Another teacher said: "My foundations in Maths are stronger after this course—I am very sure I can teach better. I realize that I was just repeating from a text, whereas now I can talk from my own knowledge, with more confidence."

Their concurrence on most issues was striking. Teachers in the class often talked over each other in their excitement, as they vigorously agreed with their colleagues' perspectives, and expressed great hope and inspiration. A teacher summarized many perspectives, saying:

> Here (at CMT-C) we feel respected. We are carriers of this new knowledge and we can change our schools. We can relate to our children better. Primary teachers usually do not feel this important. The system feels we are the ones who can do all the extra work, which teachers of older children should not do, because they are doing important work. I feel I do not have time to waste anymore. I want to take this to my school, and to everyone who will listen. I regret that I did not know this before.

The initiative has been featured in several news reports in all the major dailies since its inception. The following is a news report by Krishnan (2011), writing in the *Deccan Chronicle*, which documents children's activities in a Montessori classroom and includes teachers and the SRCT's perspectives on the partnership:

> *Four-year-old Niyaz uses a sharp knife in his school. He carefully cuts carrots into various shapes. He is capable of lifting a glass jug and placing it back after filling water in cups.*
>
> *His five-year-old friend Monica ties up the knots in the coat with ease. Making chappathi (Indian whole wheat flatbread), doing pooja (worship), and cleaning the study materials are learning activities for kids like Niyaz and Monica.*
>
> *Like them over hundreds of students in various Chennai Corporation schools enjoy their classes taught under the Montessori system. The classes are run by a group of women under the banner "Sriramcharan trust."*
>
> *The women's group has trained 25 committed teachers who are posted to corporation schools to enrich the self-confidence of children in 20 balwadi and seven Chennai corporation centres.*
>
> *Six-year-old Grace prefers her school to her home. "I get to play more here than at home," she says. Grace also learns the basics of maths, English and science subjects just by playing in her colourful class-room.*
>
> *Teacher Nithya Kalyani said that children would behave well if they were respected. She said, "Many of us love children but fail to respect them. In Montessori system the teacher doesn't 'teach' children but assists them. The teacher is supposed to observe the children and guide them to pick up their skills." She said that mothers Girija and Asha have enrolled themselves in Montessori training to become teachers after they were saw the development in their children.*
>
> *Octogenarian Padmini Gopal, who helps from the backroom of Montessori classes in corporation schools said, "There is a mis-conception the Montessori system is elitist. But this system is the right tool to break down the class system in our society. Cutting across the rich and poor divide, children mingle and get to under-stand others' problems."*
>
> *She adds that if the Montessori education is implemented in government schools, children would enjoy learning and grow with confidence.*

You may wonder why there were few dissenting views reported in this chapter. Did all teachers want this approach in their classrooms? Did all parents see it as a good system for their children? Were all children engaged by it? I had to keep reminding myself of such questions as I saw the flood of acceptance that this project elicited. In fact, that is why I felt compelled to write about it. I have worked in educational research for over 15 years now, and have studied a range of approaches that were tried out in schools. Some approaches that I considered impressive, played out briefly in schools and districts, and died a natural death, while others that I thought poor, to my dismay, won over multitudes and prospered in school systems. As a result, I have learned to reserve judgment on what is and is not a "good" educational approach, and adopt a wait and watch attitude as behooves an educational anthropologist. However, the Chennai project, which I encountered without much of an awareness of Montessori education, won me over bit by bit, just as it won over dozens of teachers, students, and parents.

It is challenging to "measure" educational outcomes at the preschool level, as children are grappling with the building blocks of numeracy and literacy, and cannot be tested with traditional assessments. The outcome studies by Lillard and others in the United States (cited in a previous section) rely on testing children in primary and secondary school, using the length of Montessori exposure as the independent variable, with student performance on tests as the dependent variable. CMT-C/Kalvi is attempting to replicate such a study in Chennai Corporation schools. However, no independent evaluations with outcome data are available to date.

We can keep debating what the ideal system for child learning and development should look like, or we can consider a system that has clear merit and significant staying power. I felt compelled to document the Chennai Montessori project because it is a symbol of what is possible for thousands of children whose parents are preoccupied with their daily financial struggles and not in a position to pay for superior schools. Many parents that I interviewed just wanted their children to know some English and be able to write exams and finish school. This was because they saw schooling as a step toward a better future—as a way out of their present socioeconomic difficulties. The Corporation stepping forward to scale up the small initiative begun by SRCT and CMT-C/Kalvi in a few schools will pave a path toward thousands of students eventually benefiting from a preschool experience that is qualitatively superior to what they would otherwise have.

The project is not without challenges. Each Montessori-certified teacher requires one full sets of preschool level Montessori material, so that she can actually transfer her learning to the classroom, and children

can fully participate in this method of learning. Although three batches
of teachers completed the CMT-C certification course, only a few
Corporation classrooms received materials within the same time frame.
The majority of teachers, though motivated and fully prepared, were
unable to use the Montessori Method due to lack of materials. The Trusts
and the Corporation were strained for the significant amount of funding
required to purchase adequate sets of materials. The project went
through a low phase, when it looked like the REAL experience would
repeat in Chennai. In REAL in Thailand, it was the capacity issue on the
part of the private partners to extend their network throughout the state
at a pace that would ensure that the program reached all public schools
quickly and with integrity to the nuanced nature of the program. In
Chennai, even that hurdle was overcome, but the high costs of scaling
up the implementation seemed insurmountable because of the cost of the
Montessori materials.

Recent news reports, however, indicate that there may be hope, as the
Corporation has announced that 30 sets of materials will be made available to schools, and more will be purchased so that the program is uniformly implemented throughout all schools with preschools and
Kindergartens in the Corporation of Chennai. Ramalingam (2012)
writes in the *Times of India* that officials of the Corporation of Chennai
announced that all 30 kindergartens are to have Montessori environments. She writes:

> There are 284 corporation schools of which 30 have kindergarten
> sections attached to primary and middle schools. Officials said 96
> corporation school teachers have been trained in Montessori
> methodology. ... "Material delivery will begin in the second week
> of June and classes will commence from July," an official said. ...
> In all, there would be 30 such modules, each costing ₹ one lakh.[12]
> It will encompass mats, wooden toys, low level desks and other
> material. This would be entirely be funded by the corporation. ...
> Montessori education is not new in corporation schools. The
> movement towards this type of education began five years ago
> when the corporation in partnership with a few non-governmental
> organizations introduced it in its schools at VP Koil Street,
> Mylapore, Saidapet and Velachery. Put together, there are ten
> Montessori modules in these schools. "In the last few years, we
> have seen a surge in admissions to class 1 in schools that have
> Montessori modules in their kindergarten sections," officials said.

The project has won the support of Corporation officials, teachers, and parents. It has engaged students in every classroom that it is currently implemented in. The Corporation Montessori project has the makings of a lasting systemic initiative. The next year is crucial for the initiative as it passes into the hands of Corporation teachers, with Trust partners likely to take on supervisory and guiding roles rather than teaching roles in classrooms.

Chapter 5 dwells on the implications of the case studies of Middle Start and the Montessori project for educational quality, scale, and sustainability. It connects the literature on PPPs reviewed in the first chapter with emerging views on social enterprise in Western Europe, which see PPPs, or more specifically PSPs, as a format for sustainable delivery of quality public services. Though the literature on PSPs and social enterprises does not directly address issues of public education and its reform, I argue in the concluding chapter that the framework provided by the European movement can be usefully applied to education, of course with caveats.

NOTES

1. I carried out intensive field visits from 2005-2009. Post-2009, I continued to interview Trust representatives and the lead teacher at Saidapet on major developments up until April, 2012. The latest developments in the project are reported from news reports in national newspapers (the last available being May 2012).
2. I did not get an opportunity to interview parents at Thondiarpet, as it was the newest school in the project and I visited it the least.
3. The review does not include descriptions of Montessori classrooms and materials. Please refer Paula Polk Lillard (1996) for an excellent discussion of the method at work in classrooms.
4. Cited in Lillard (2005, p. 10).
5. I was present at the conference.
6. IAS stands for Indian Administrative Service, including an elite cadre of bureaucrats who head government divisions throughout India.
7. Rishi Valley is a reputed school in Andhra Pradesh in India. It is part of the group of schools run by the Krishnamurthi Foundation of India (KFI), a not-for-profit organization.
8. Refer the detailed discussion of ABL in Tamil Nadu under the heading Experimental/Policy-driven in Chapter 2. ABL was implemented in Grades 1–5. The Montessori project worked with the preschool and kindergarten

sections of several schools that were also implementing ABL in the primary grades.

9. Roti is Indian flat bread. *Bindi*s are dots that many women wear for decorative reasons in the middle of their forehead in India. Pulses are edible legumes that can be ground to a powder with a mortar and pestle. Sieving, pouring, and other activities that mimic adult work in the kitchen are taught to children as part of the exercises of practical life.

10. Refer Lillard's (1996) *Montessori Today: A Comprehensive Approach to Education from Birth to Childhood*, for detailed descriptions of the sequence of activities presented in a Montessori preschool classroom.

11. The course was run over two summers and Saturdays during the school year. Teachers preferred that they not be named. Hence names are not used in this section.

12. One lakh is ₹100,000; $1 (US) was roughly equal to ₹55 at the time of writing. The cost of the one set of Montessori materials translates to approximately US$1800 at the time of going to press.

5

Resolving the Paradox

Teaching and learning, and their betterment (as seen in the previous examples), required several stakeholders to come together, experiment, and keep refining their work to really influence what ultimately happens in classrooms. At Owen Middle School, part of Middle Start, we saw the many points of entry needed to work toward the central issues of teaching and learning: good coaching; district support; leadership, both from administrators and teachers; and involvement from teachers, parents, and students. The content of the reform was decided after weighing in district requirements, the model's guidelines, the school's needs, the coach's vision, and the perspectives of the school's constituents. The chosen direction had to be buttressed by high-quality professional development, on-site experimentation, reflection, review, and then carefully chosen next steps. As teaching and learning began to change and improve, stakeholders had to consider whether the change was school-wide, and whether they could sow the seeds for it to continue over the long term. Model developers had to look across school sites to consider the lessons learned and select what would lead to a more efficient and replicable approach, to saturate systems, and grow the initiative. They had to develop institutions at different levels, or help existing institutions develop greater capacity, to refine their work, reach more schools, and share their learning with others in the initiative. As the webs were built, first among schools and coaches, then among districts, and finally with the State, connecting varied sponsors, implementers, researchers, and school constituents, those responsible for the initiative had to be careful that it kept its focus on the quality of teaching and learning and on scale and sustainability.

Though on a smaller scale, CMT-C/Kalvi and Sri Ramacharan Charitable Trust experienced a similar trajectory. The first issue of educational quality was solved easier than it was in Middle Start, as they proposed a tried-and-tested method of early childhood education, the Montessori Method. Those familiar with this method know that it is scarcely touched over the 100 years it has been in existence, and its proponents believe that it has all the elements for building conceptual, sensorial, and practical knowledge in young children. Thus, the content of professional development and classroom-level implementation were mostly uniform across the schools in the project, and did not have the variegation of Middle Start. However, the project initially faced issues of variations in teacher buy-in, as many Corporation teachers comfortable with their ways of teaching were aghast at the prospect of learning a new, very detailed, very different system. Principals and parents also questioned whether this system, in which rote instruction was completely absent, would prepare their children for the higher grades, where direct instruction and rote learning were the predominant modes of teaching and learning. The Corporation of Chennai, though willing to expand the project, took some years to decide that it would provide time and funds for every preschool and kindergarten teacher to become a certified Montessori teacher. The implementers are currently addressing the challenges of raising funds to purchase materials, providing in-school coaching, and documenting and refining the program. Sustaining the work in existing schools is proceeding well due to the excellent support that teachers have from the Trusts.

I have often wondered if a third partner, in the form of a foundation (similar to the WKKF in Middle Start) could have helped spur the process of refinement and consolidation through a multiyear grant to the Trusts. This support would have reduced the pressure on the organizations to generate funds on a yearly basis, and focus instead on reflection, refinement, expansion, and documentation.

I hope my words have helped paint a picture of the nuanced, difficult, multifaceted task that education reform is. Middle Start and the Montessori project came to be because of the vision, commitment, and hard work of their implementers. Both public and private partners had the goal of providing students who could not afford to pay for a great education, great public schools. Their zeal is what catalyzed initially small movements to grow throughout public systems. A critical point is that the implementers were purely driven by their interest in an excellent and equitable education for disadvantaged children. Three other projects discussed in Chapter 2, REAL in Thailand, Math and Science Partnership in Puerto Rico, and ABL in Tamil Nadu, India,[1] also mirrored the same zeal and infused energy into depleted public systems in other parts of the world.

What if these partners had instead been driven by self-interest? Or an interest in building their reputations, their institutions, and balancing their books? Would the quality of what happens in a classroom be the focus? Would the teachers who didn't want to do something different receive a fair hearing and time to consider other methods? Would schools have the option to reflect on and choose their path to improvement or have a "one-size fits all" approach imposed on them? Would implementers choose to fix the student or fix the system?

The examples of Edison School's focus on basic skills as an educational strategy and the Philadelphia takeover's need to show rapid improvement in test scores, both discussed in Chapter 2, are evidence that entities with other pressures, than the improvement of teaching and learning, may not be in the best position to act as reformers of public systems. The demands of reforming large systems are huge, and raising test scores is an unpredictable business, even when things go well. To cite Garcia, Barber and Molnar (2009), who studied EMO-managed schools in the US:

> As profit-seeking enterprises, EMOs respond to the incentives provided by the legal and financial systems in which they operate. The bottom line is that for-profit schools must spend less than they collect. In so doing, EMO-managed charter schools face an internal conflict between cost savings and quality of education. (p. 1370)

Perhaps, then, an educational for-profit organization could conduct remedial programs within large systems? After all, as seen in the Balsakhi case in Chapter 2, they are simple, replicable, measurable, and may raise achievement, at least in the short run. However, the trend in education reform is away from remedial education and "fixing" underperforming students. Entities as diverse as the World Bank, the National Staff Development Council in the United States, and proponents of de-tracking are urging reformers to think systemically, and first figure out what ails systems and then devise ways of addressing the problems.

Perhaps then, the best way to profit from public education is to contract with the government to build and maintain schools or carry out logistical services, as long as they are unrelated to teaching and learning. It may well be that for-profit entities, with their efficient methods and economies of scale, suit such areas of school operations and ease the burden on public systems by performing them well.

Several countries in Europe have realized that PPPs are essential to their growth and well-being, as the burden of delivering public services is too large for governments alone. There is a growing trend of PSP in these countries (initiated by governments of countries such as Italy, Ireland, Scotland, Germany, and Poland), where critical public services are formally contracted out to what they term "third sector" organizations within the voluntary and nonprofit sector. Funded by the European Union in some instances, these partnerships are helping governments provide healthcare, housing, and other services in an efficient and equitable manner.

The literature on PSPs intersects with the one on social enterprises, as the European experiment with PSPs has invited a large group of third sector organizations (neither public, nor private for-profit, and therefore composing a "third" sector) in partnerships with governments. Some of these voluntary and not-for-profit organizations have grown into social enterprises, which are able to sustain themselves through generating revenue through the delivery of services, while staying focused on the public interest. Social enterprises are emerging as a new paradigm in several countries. Europe and the United States are actively experimenting with this field and several researchers in both regions are engaged in conceptualizing and documenting the field. Social enterprises are also gaining ground in developing countries in Asia and South America. In many cases, social enterprises are the "private" part of public–private partnerships, as they work via a contract or on a fee-for-service basis to deliver public services.

There are interesting differences between European and American social enterprises, as the ones in Europe work within the social economy while those in America mostly within the market economy. I discuss social enterprises in some detail later, as a trend within PSPs. Unfortunately, I was not able to identify any examples of education reform through PSPs or social enterprises in the literature. I close this chapter and the book with a discussion of possible implications of PSPs for education reform.

PUBLIC SOCIAL PARTNERSHIPS

Most writers on PSPs refer the cooperative movement in Italy as the genesis of this trend in Europe. Vanek (2001) chronicles the development of Italian cooperatives and identifies increased strain on the government, both financially and in terms of service delivery, as the reason for the development of cooperatives. She writes:

Italian social cooperatives provided services to the "economically weaker layers of society" as Italy, like other western European nations which had developed extensive welfare state programs, sought to diminish the financial burden of such programs. They were also able to make a dent in the unemployment problem, which by the 1980's was extensive in Italy as well as other Western European countries. Certain marginal groups of the unemployed were given work in the cooperatives.

Vanek writes that the first cooperatives began in the 1970s, and the movement grew rapidly in the 1980s. A law was passed in 1991, embedding this form in policy. The debate that led to the law provided the following framework for social cooperatives:

1. The legal form of the organization must be a cooperative and it must have a social or community function. The term "social cooperatives" distinguished these organizations and the nature of their work from regular cooperatives, which mainly benefited their own members.
2. Social cooperatives must service the local community, especially those needing social welfare services and those who were unemployed. The law clarified two forms: social service cooperatives in healthcare, care of the elderly, and education; and creation of employment for those with physical or mental health issues, drug users, alcoholics, criminals, and troubled youth.
3. They must have a membership, among others, of "normally employed working members; special workers, handicapped in some way, required to comprise 30 percent of the cooperatives dealing with unemployment; volunteers, whose numbers and scope were limited; and persons providing financial support" (Vanek, 2001).

Social cooperatives received tax waivers and reductions, and could pay members who were physically challenged at a lower rate than the minimum wage. Vanek states that this framework applied to all social cooperatives in Italy, but their governance was devolved to regional levels, so that local needs and governance were synchronized. Government bodies were the main clients of social cooperatives and a major portion of their funding came through contracts with government agencies for carrying out social welfare services.

PSPs have taken root in many countries within the European Union in the last decade, including France, Ireland, the United Kingdom, Finland, and Belgium, according to Defourny and Nyssenss (2008). Some examples of PSPs from Scotland include: support services for people with learning disabilities, commissioning of services to children and families, and expanding current levels of employment of people with disabilities. According to the website of the Scotland project, there are three stages in their approach (Scottish Government, 2011):

1. Third sector organizations working with public sector purchasers to design a service.
2. A consortium of public sector and third sector organizations participating in a short-term pilot, helping to refine service delivery parameters.
3. The service is further developed to maximize community benefit before being competitively tendered.

An evaluation of the Scotland PSP's work finds that social enterprises definitely add value to the delivery of social services. McDonald, Wilson, and Jack (n.d.), assessors of the initiative, state:

The Scottish Government has emphasized that, for the public sector, the social economy sector's proven ability to innovate and experience in working with particular client groups can provide the opportunity for wider social benefit when the two work together to deliver public services. These wider social benefits represent social added value for the public sector.

The lessons learned from the pilots are instructive, as they point to a process-oriented, long-term view of partnerships that emphasizes shared perspectives, co-planning, and capacity-building to carry out the work well:

1. All participants in the PSP, from both sectors, must buy into a shared definition of the problem, and approaches to solutions.
2. The PSP needs to have high levels of public sector support from civil servants and senior officers, who in turn ensure that the needs of the work are met at different stages of its implementation.
3. There are differences in the working culture of the public and social economy sectors, and a co-planning approach is needed to

problem-solve, set up processes and procedures, and work out funding arrangements.

4. Clarity of the focus of the PSP, funding proportionate to the scope and scale of the work, and providing services with the client's needs in mind are central to the success of the PSP.

5. Both sectors need to build their capacity to accommodate to the needs of the partnership through additional training and development of their staff.

6. Both sectors need to build bridges and keep communication going in order to ensure that the new modes of delivering services are nurtured appropriately.

7. It takes time to build shared definitions, compatible work cultures, develop capacity, and establish communication channels. Resources and time need to be allocated for the building of the partnership which facilitates the work (McDonald et al., pp. 2–4).

The literature on funding arrangements in the PSP format is in general agreement that in Europe public sector agencies usually contract with third sector organizations for the delivery of public services through entering into a PSP. Public funds are allocated to the work, and the public and third sector organizations need to gauge whether the funds are proportionate to the work, whether the public sector is saving by investing in the PSP, and the third sector is gaining by carrying out the work. Third sector organizations use the revenue gained from carrying out these services to fund work related to their mission. The revenue is not kept as profit for any individual or shared between the members of the organization, unless the organization is a cooperative, in which case limited distribution of profits is allowed. Thus, in Europe, the term "social enterprise," as the goals of the organization are socially inclined and the methods of delivering good-quality public services are based on innovative, cost-saving methods, implying a spirit of entrepreneurship.

EMES (The Emergence of Social Enterprise in Europe) Project begun in 1996 with funding from the European Union specializes in research on the third sector, with an emphasis on social enterprises and PSPs. EMES defines social enterprise as including:

1. A continuous activity producing goods and/or selling services;
2. A high degree of autonomy;
3. A significant level of economic risk;
4. A minimum amount of paid work;

5. An explicit aim to benefit the community;
6. An initiative launched by a group of citizens;
7. A decision-making power not based on capital ownership;
8. A participatory nature, which involves the persons affected by the activity;
9. Limited profit distribution (Defourny, 2001, pp.16–18, cited in Kerlin, 2006, p. 3).

In the United States, however, writes Kerlin (2006), the concept of social enterprise is more focused "on enterprise for the sake of revenue generation than definitions elsewhere." She writes that social enterprise includes a wide spectrum of organizations, including

> ...profit-oriented businesses engaged in socially beneficial activities (corporate philanthropies or corporate social responsibility) to dual-purpose businesses that mediate profit goals with social objectives (hybrids) to nonprofit organizations engaged in mission-supporting commercial activity (social purpose organizations). For social purpose organizations, mission-supporting commercial activity may include only revenue generation that supports other programming. ...Social enterprise engaged in by nonprofits may take on a number of different organizational forms including internal commercial ventures, for-profit and nonprofit subsidiaries, and partnerships with business including cause-related marketing. (p.2)

Defourny and Nyssens (2008) also present a similar differentiation between European and American social enterprises:

> (European) social enterprises indeed combine income from sales or fees from users with public subsidies linked to their social mission and private donations and/or volunteering. This clearly contrasts with a strong US tendency to define social enterprises only as non-profit organizations more oriented towards the market and developing "earned income strategies" as a response to decreasing public subsidies and to the limits of private grants from foundations. (p. 5)

In a recent edited volume on social enterprise in different parts of the world, Kerlin (2009) invited researchers from Western and East–Central Europe, the United States, Southeast Asia, Japan, parts of Africa, and

Argentina to discuss the social contexts in which social enterprises emerged in these regions. Each chapter discusses the historical backgrounds, variation in forms of social enterprises, governance, and types of work undertaken by such enterprises in varied national and socioeconomic contexts. Kerlin concludes that social enterprises are rapidly becoming an accepted approach to fulfilling a social mission through a revenue-generating structure. She observes that pilots and small initiatives at the grassroots level developed by such enterprises pay great attention to the socioeconomic needs of a local community, therefore making the social enterprise an integral partner in the growth and development of the community. She concludes that public initiatives can effectively expand and replicate the work of social enterprises, as often they meet important social needs, and are rooted within their socioeconomic milieu.

Defourny and Nyssens (2008) also acknowledge the variations and local moorings of social enterprises, and observe that the term "social enterprise has broadened with the mushrooming of partnerships on both sides of the Atlantic, Japan, and Korea since the late 1990s. They state that the usage ranges from voluntary activism to corporate social responsibility, but emphasize that the European definition of social entrepreneurship is only about the third or not-for-profit sector, although they acknowledge that the American interpretation of "blended value creation (profits alongside social value)" is gaining ground. The EMES stance as summarized by them is as follows:

Social enterprises are not-for-profit private organizations providing goods or services directly related to their explicit aim to benefit the community. They rely on a collective dynamic involving various types of stakeholders in their governing bodies, they place a high value on their autonomy and they bear economic risks linked to their activity. (p.6)

Defourny and Nyssens also identify the integral role of social enterprises in Europe in carrying out public schemes related to work integration or bringing in the unemployed, differently abled, and others who find it difficult to find employment into productive roles. They state that social enterprises are almost synonymous with employment-generation schemes in many parts of Europe. They write (2008):

Indeed, the persistence of structural unemployment among some groups, the limits of traditional active labour market policies and the need for more active and innovative integration policies have

naturally raised questions concerning the role that social enter-
prises could play in combating unemployment and fostering
employment growth. Precisely, the main objective of work inte-
gration social enterprises is to help low qualified unemployed
people, who are at risk of permanent exclusion from the labour
market. (p. 8)

In an overview of the emerging field of venture philanthropy in
Europe, a funding approach to grow and sustain social enterprises, Ochs
(2009, p.5) writes that social enterprises are seen to mainly operate in
the fields of work integration (training and integration of unemployed
persons); personal services (child-care services, services for elderly
people, aid for disadvantaged people); and local development in disadvantaged areas. The article states that there is a range of sectors in which
such enterprises operate in the UK, including health, social care, renew-
able energy, and recycling. In Sweden and in France child-care services
are initiated and managed by parents due to shortage in their provision
by governments. In Ireland, social enterprises are engaged in local
development; and in Greece, such enterprises take the form of agro-
tourist cooperatives in remote areas.

My search of the literature for research on social enterprises focused
on education, specifically public school reform, yielded sparse results.
Teach for America, a not-for-profit organization based in the United
States, has successfully branched out all over the world as Teach for All
(TFA), with branches in India, Spain, Brazil, and many other countries.
TFA describes itself as a social enterprise, focused on the improvement
of teaching and learning through bringing in fresh minds into the teaching profession, and building their capacity to become educational leaders within schools and systems.[2]However, TFA has been critiqued by
many for the limited preparation and experience of TFA teachers, short
duration of their engagement in classrooms, limited influence on school
systems, and tall claims (see Sims, 2010, for a detailed overview of
research on TFA's engagement with schools). While a detailed discussion of TFA is outside the scope of this chapter, a major difference
between TFA and Middle Start and the Montessori project is the long-
term, systemic nature of the latter and the limited, classroom-based
engagement of TFA.

The review of literature on social enterprises shows that they are
positioned as a blend of public and private, as they focus on social goals,
but rely on an entrepreneurial approach to fulfill their goals in times

when governments and foundations have limited resources. In Europe, social enterprises are regulated by legal frameworks that recognize their unique contributions in service delivery, and close off any opportunities for misuse through careful delineation of what is and is not a social enterprise. EMES is funded by the European Commission to conduct formative and summative research on the field of social enterprise, and guide its growth in an informed manner. The regulations, research, and social enterprise networks provide an infrastructure within which this movement is rapidly progressing in Europe. This indicates that any such experiment in a country outside the EU requires a similar infrastructure, as the US trend indicates that a market economy does not regulate social enterprises to the same extent, and may not provide the balance needed between self-interest and the public interest. It is important to note that social enterprises need appropriate regulation in order to be effective in PPPs.

It is interesting that there were no easily retrievable in-depth case studies of social enterprises in action that illustrated the linkages between governance, mission, partner roles, and the process of carrying out their work. Insider perspectives, analyses of the contributions, challenges, and lessons learned of these initiatives are few and far between. Does this imply that anthropologists and sociologists have not yet trained their sights on them? It may be an error of omission on my part, but clearly this area could benefit from more published work on the inner workings of social enterprises, perspectives of stakeholders, clients, public sponsors, and others such entities; and answers to the question of whether and what kinds of value they add, and how and why. It is disappointing that this literature does not talk about the reform of public education, and if social entrepreneurship is a good fit for education reform.

IMPLICATIONS OF PSPS FOR EDUCATION REFORM

Some authors have emphatically denounced PPPs in education in India (Narayan, 2010; Datta, 2009; Kumar, 2008) on several grounds. Although Narayan (2010) delineates variations of PPPs, and emphasizes that they cannot be discussed as a monolithic concept, he argues that private and public schools should remain distinct, as private engagement in public schools represents a blurring of identities and duties. Datta (2009) is trenchant in her critique of PPPs in development, focusing only on the privatization aspect and the prospect of exploitation of public institutions and the public by private entities under the guise of partnership. Kumar (2008) goes even further to say that PPPs represent India's emergent neoliberal leanings and threaten to shrink and marginalize important functions of the government. He cautions strongly against nongovernmental organizations (NGOs) playing any role in public schools, as he feels the rise of the what he terms the "corporate NGO," large, well-funded NGOs, increase the risk of privatization without in any way improving public systems. Kumar refers to PPPs as an ideology, rather than a vehicle for partnership. However, his own highly ideological critique of partnerships undermines his argument, as he focuses on one of the greatest perils of PPPs—the threat of privatization—and ignores other facets.

Applying the framework discussed in Chapter 2, of scope, scale, method, and motive, helps gain a nuanced understanding of PPPs. It helps to deconstruct this sweeping term so that the debate on its merits and demerits can go past the ideological divide, in which it is becoming mired. Applying the framework gives us the opportunity to identify PSP-based initiatives like the Math and Science Partnership in Puerto Rico, ABL in Tamil Nadu, REAL in Thailand, Middle Start in Michigan, and the Montessori project in Chennai, and acknowledge the fruitful partnerships forged among public officials, educational organizations, foundations, teachers, students, and parents within these initiatives.

The idea behind this book was to present a balanced picture which brings to light the perils and simultaneously unpacks the promise of PPPs in education. The book has also raised another critical question: Can bona fide NGOs, concerned citizens, and parents *not* participate in improving their government or public schools and systems? Does their presence and work in these systems only signify a desire to take over and privatize or diminish and marginalize public systems? Can they not rightfully play a role in reviving these ailing systems and making them equal to the task of educating children without being suspected of trying to "privatize" these systems? Political scientists hold that community participation is a critical component of democratic systems, and can enhance the capacity of public systems (Stone, Henig, Jones, & Pierannunzi, 2001). This book has amply acknowledged the perils of PPPs, and sharply delineated where the line falls in terms of scope, scale, method, and motive regarding who is and who is not an appropriate partner for public systems. Ideological critiques for and against PPPs, or any other concept for that matter, mitigate the potential for a balanced view of any issue, especially a complex issue like reforming public education.

Perhaps the European iteration of the PPP, the PSP, in which public authorities and social enterprises work together through a mutually agreed framework for a well-defined cause, will slow down even ideologues from throwing out the proverbial baby with the bathwater. I invite educationists of varied stripes to participate in a dialogue on this approach, as PSPs have worked well within what EMES calls the social economy of the European Union, and have been tried in India and elsewhere (but without applying this label). So, all things considered, are PSPs ultimately an answer to the problem of lackluster reforms in public education? I would hate to end my book with the overused disclaimer that we need more research before we can conclusively support educational partnerships. The body of work reviewed, including my original cases and studies by other researchers, shows that PSPs can attain significant levels of quality and scale in the long term. Sustainability remains tricky, given the complex policy and funding equations in most school systems. Despite this caveat, it is clear that there is a complementarity, a yin–yang, between committed private entities and public systems. Their synergy can revitalize public education.

NOTES

1. Chennai is the capital of Tamil Nadu, a large state in south India. The Montessori project works with the preschool and kindergarten grades of schools within the Corporation of Chennai. The ABL program is implemented in Grades 1–5 of state-run schools in Chennai and throughout Tamil Nadu.

2. See http://teachforallnetwork.org/aboutus_history.html to learn more about TFA.

Bibliography

Akaguri, L. (2011). Quality low-fee private schools for the rural poor: Perception or reality? Evidence from Southern Ghana. *CREATE Pathways to Access Series, Research Monograph Number69*, 44. Centre for International Education, Department of Education, University of Sussex, Falmer, UK. ISBN 0-901881-82-1.

Akila, R. (2009). A trigger for change in primary education: An evaluation of ABL in Tamil Nadu, 2009. Tamil Nadu: Sarva Shiksha Abhiyan. Retrieved on June 24, 2012 from http://www.ssa.tn.nic.in/CBE.htm.

Aladjem, D., & Borman, K. (2006). An introduction to comprehensive school reform. In D. Aladjem & K. Borman (Eds.), *Examining comprehensive school reform*. Washington, DC: Urban Institute Press.

Anandalakshmi, S. (2007). Activity-based learning: A report on an innovative method in Tamil Nadu. TamilNadu: Sarva Shiksha Abhiyan. Retrieved from http://www.ssa.tn.nic.in/Docu/ABL-Report-by-Dr. Anandhalakshmi.pdf on March 17, 2010.

Balfanz, R. (2009). *Putting middle grades students on the graduation path: A policy and practice brief*. Baltimore, MD: Everyone Graduates Center and Talent Development Middle Grades Program.

Ball, S.J., & Youdell, D. (2007). *Hidden privatization in public education*. Brussels, Belgium: Education International.

Banerjee, A., Cole, S., Duflo, E., & Linden, L. (2005), Remedying education: Evidence from two randomized experiments in India. *NBER Working Paper No. 11904*. Retrieved from http://econ-www.mit.edu/files/804 on January 9, 2011.

Bangalore Bureau. (2012). Children of a lesser cut. *The Hindu*, July 18, 2012. Retrieved on July 18, 2012 from http://www.thehindu.com/news/cities/bangalore/children-of-a-lesser-cut/article3650505.ece.

Bartlett, A., & Jatiket, M. (2003). Getting REAL in Thai schools. *Pesticides News No. 61* (September 2003), 6–7.

Blazer, C. (2010). *Research comparing charter schools and traditional schools*. Miami, FL: Office of Assessment, Research, and Data Analysis, Miami-Dade County Public Schools.

Bodilly, S.J. (1996). *Lessons from new American schools: Development corporation's demonstration phase*. Santa Monica, CA: RAND.

———. (1998). *Lessons from new American schools' scale-up phase: Prospects for bringing designs to multiple schools*. Santa Monica, CA: RAND.

Berman, G., Hewes, G., Overman, L., & Brown, S. (2003). Comprehensive school reform and achievement: A meta-analysis. *Review of Educational Research, 73* (2), 125–130.

Bosker, R., Creemers, B., & Stringfield, S. (1999). *Enhancing educational equity, excellence and efficiency*. The Netherlands: Kluwer Academic Press.

CREDO—Center for Research on Education Outcomes. (2009). *Multiple choice: Charter school performance in 16 states*. Stanford, CA: Stanford University.

Casas, M. (2011). *Enhancing student learning in middle school*. New York: Routledge.

Center for Policy Research in Education. (1998). States and districts and comprehensive school reform. CPRE Policy Briefs, RB-24, May 1998.

Chubb, J.E., & Moe, T.M. (1990). *Politics, markets and America's schools*. Washington, DC: The Brookings Institution.

Corbett, D., & Wilson, B. (2007). *Middle start: Implementation, impact, and lessons learned 2003-6*. New York: Academy for Educational Development.

Corbett, H.D., Fancsali, C., Gopalan, P., Weinbaum, A., & Wilson, B.L. (2006). Partnerships in middle grades comprehensive school reform. In D.K. Aladjem & K. Borman (Eds.), *Examining comprehensive school reform* (pp. 247–284). Washington DC: Urban Institute Press.

Datta, A. (2009). Public-private partnerships in India: A case for reform? *Economic and Political Weekly, XLIV*(33), pp. 73–78, August 15, 2009.

Deccan Chronicle. (2012). Private schools ignore 25% free quota to poor. *Deccan Chronicle*, Retrieved on July 19, 2012 from http://www.deccanchronicle.com/channels/cities/regions/karimnagar/private-schools-ignore-25-free-quota-poor-223.

Defoumy, J. (2001). Introduction: From third sector to social enterprise. In C. Barzaga and J. Defoumy (Eds.), *The emergence of social enterprise*. London: Routledge.

Defourny, J., & Nyssens, M. (2008). Social enterprise in Europe: Recent trends and developments. *Social Enterprise Journal, 4*(3), 202–228

Dhawan, H. (2012). Centre needs ₹2.3 lakh crore to fund RTE initiative. *Times of India*, April 13, 2012. Retrieved on July 15, 2012 from http://articles.timesofindia.indiatimes.com/2012-04-13/india/31337176_1_lakh-teachers-rte-teacher-ratio.

DiCarlo, M. (2011). *A "summary opinion" of the Hoxby NYC charter study*. Boulder, CO: National Education Policy Center, University of Colorado at Boulder.

Dohrmann, K.R. (2003). *Outcomes for students in a Montessori program: A longitudinal study of the experience in the Milwaukee public schools*. Rochester, NY: Association Montessori Internationale. Retrieved on September 10, 2010 from http://www.montessori-ami.org.

Dohrmann, K.R., Nishida, T., Gartner, A., Lipsky, D., & Grimm, K. (2007). High school outcomes for students in a public Montessori program. *Journal of Research in Childhood Education, 22*, 205–217.

Education Commission of the States (2010). *Compulsory school age require-ments*. Denver, CO: Education Commission of the States.

Elmore, R. (1996). Getting to scale with good educational practice. *Harvard Educational Review, 66* (1), 1–26.

Elmore, R. F., & McLaughlin, M. W. (1988). *Steady work: Policy, practice and re-educational dissemination and change*. Santa Monica, CA: RAND Corporation.

Fink, D. (2000). *Good schools, real schools: Why school reform doesn't last*. New York: Teachers College Press.

Friedman, M. (1955). The role of government in education. In R. A. Solo (Ed.), *Economics and the public interest* (pp. 123–144). New Brunswick, NJ: Rutgers University Press.

———. (1962). *Capitalism and freedom*. Chicago: University of Chicago Press.

Fullan, M. (1990). Beyond implementation. *Curriculum Implementation, 202* (2), 137–139.

———. (2009). Large scale reform comes of age. *Journal of Educational Change, 10*(2), 101–113.

Garcia, D.R., Barber, R., & Molnar, A. (2009). Profiting from public education: Education management organizations and student achievement. *Teachers College Record 111*(5), 1352–1379.

Gardner, H. (1983/2003). *Frames of mind. The theory of multiple intelligences*. New York: Basic Books.

———. (1993). *Multiple intelligences: The theory in practice*. New York: Basic Books.

Gomez, M. (2004). *Systemic education reform in a large, complex educational system: Lessons learned*. Paris: UNESCO.

Gopalan, P., & Jessup, P. (2001). *Finding a balance: Approaches to middle start technical assistance in school year 1999-2000*. Studies of Middle Start school improvement. New York: Academy for Educational Development.

Gopalan, P., West, T., Montesano, P., & Hoelscher, S. (2005). Using research to refine school improvement in the middle grades. In M. Caskey (Ed.), *Making a difference: Action research in middle level education*. Greenwich, CT: Information Age Publishing.

Harvard Educational Review. (2006). From the Editors: Mayoral takeovers in education: A recipe for progress or peril? *Harvard Educational Review*. Retrieved February July 19, 2010, from http://www.hepg.org/her/abstract/6.

Henig, J.R., & Rich, W.C. (2004). *Mayors in the middle: Politics, race, and mayoral control of urban schools*. Princeton, NJ: Princeton University Press.

Hentschtke, G.C., Oschman, S., & Snell, L. (2002). *Education management organizations: Growing a for-profit education industry with choice, competi-tion, and innovation*. Los Angeles, CA: Reason Foundation.

Herman, R., Aladjem, D., McMahon, P., Masem, E., Mulligan, I., O'Malley, A., Quinones, S., Reeve, A., & Woodruff, D. (1999). *An educators' guide to schoolwide reform*. Washington, DC: American Institutes for Research.

Hess, F.M., & Manno, B.V. (2011). *Customized schooling: Beyond whole school reform.* Cambridge, MA: Harvard Education Press

Holfester, C. (2008). *The Montessori method. EBSCO research starters.* Ipswich, MA: EBSCO Publishing Inc.

Hopkins, D. (2011). *Powerful learning: Taking education reform to scale.* Melbourne: Department of Early Childhood Education.

Howe, K. (2004). A critique of experimentalism. *Qualitative Inquiry, 10* (4), 42–61.

Hoxby, C. (2004). Achievement in charter schools and regular public schools in the United States: *Understanding the differences, program on education policy and governance.* Working Paper. Cambridge, MA: Harvard University.

Hoxby, C.M., Murarka, S., & Kang, J. (2009). *How New York City's charter schools affect achievement.* Cambridge, MA: New York City Charter Schools Evaluation Project.

Hoy, W., & Dipaola, M. (2009). Preface. In W. H. Dipaola (Ed.), *Studies in school improvement.* Charlotte, NC: Information Age Publishing Inc.

Indian Montessori Foundation. (n.d.). *About Montessor—Montessori in India.* Chennai, India: Indian Montessori Foundation. Retrieved on July 5, 2011 from http://www.montessori-india.org/index.html.

Indian Montessori Center. (2012). *The valedictory function for the 20th batch of Centre for Montessori Training-Chennai (CMT-C).* Bangalore, India: Indian Montessori Center. Retrieved on July 5, 2012 from http://indianmontessoric-entre.org/index.php?option=com_content&view=article&id=189.

Jackson, A.W., & Davis, G.A. (2000). *Turning points 2000: Educating adolescents in the 21st century.* New York: Teachers College Press.

Jefferson, T. (1806). *Sixth annual message.* Excerpted from a compilation of the messages and papers of the Presidents prepared under the direction of the Joint Committee on printing, of the House and Senate pursuant to an Act of the Fifty-Second Congress of the United States. New York: Bureau of National Literature, Inc., 1897 Retrieved on July 29, 2010 from http://avalon. law.yale.edu/19th_century/jeffmes6.asp.

Jha, P.S., & Parvathi, P. (2010). Right to education act: Critical gaps and challenges. *Economic and Political Weekly, xlv*(13), 20–23, March 27, 2010.

Jin, Y., & Zhang, H. (2008). Research on the costs of running compulsory education standards: Comparison of compulsory education internationally. *International Education Studies 1*(3, August 2008), 108–111.

J-PAL—Abdul Latif Jameel Poverty Action Lab. (n.d.). *Balsakhi remedial tutoring in Vadodara and Mumbai, India.* Cambridge, MA: Abdul Latif Jameel Poverty Action Lab. Retrieved on January 9, 2011 from http://www.poverty-actionlab.org/evaluation/balsakhi-remedial-tutoring-vadodara-and-mumbai-india.

———. (2006). *Making schools work for marginalized children: Evidence from an inexpensive and effective program in India.* Policy Briefcase No. 2 (November 2006). Massachusetts Institute of Technology: Abdul Latif

Jameel Poverty Action Lab. Retrieved on January 9, 2011 from www.povertyactionlab.org/sites/default/files/publications/26_Policy_Briefcase_2.pdf.

Juvonen, J., Le, V., Kaganoff, T., Augustine, C., & Constant, L. (2004). *Focus on the wonder years: Challenges facing the American middle school.* Santa Monica, CA: RAND Corporation.

Kantamara, P., Hallinger, P., & Jatiket, M. (2006). Scaling-up educational reform in Thailand: Context, collaboration, networks and change. *An Educational Leadership and Policy Journal, special issue: Curricular Reforms in Southeast Asia—Planning and Changing, 37*(1&2), 5–23.

Kasak, D. (2004). What middle grades need. *American School Board Journal, 191* (5), 44–45.

Kerlin, J.A. (2006). Social Enterprise in the United States and Europe: Understanding and Learning from the Differences. *Voluntas 17*(3), 247–263.

Kerlin. J. (2009). *Social enterprise: A global comparison.* Medford, MA: Tufts University Press.

Kilgore, S. (2006). The development of comprehensive school reform models. In D. Aladjem & K. Borman (Eds.), *Examining comprehensive school reform* (pp. 11–32). Washington, DC: Urban Institute Press.

Krishnan, P. (2011). Montessori system a hit among school children. *Deccan Chronicle*, August 29, 2011. Retrieved on July 5, 2012 from http://www.deccanchronicle.com/channels/cities/chennai/montessori-system-hit-among-school-children-017.

Kumar, K. (2008). Partners in education? *Economic and Political Weekly*, January 19, 2008, pp. 8–11.

Kumar, P. (2012). SSA-RTE leaves HRD Ministry in dire straits. *Deccan Herald*, May 3, 2012. Retrieved on July 14 from http://www.deccanherald.com/content/246820/ssa-rte-leaves-hrd-ministry.html

LaRocque, N. (2008). *Public-private partnerships in basic education: An international review.* UK: CfBT Education Trust.

Lee, V., Smith, J., Perry, T., & Smylie, M. (1999). *Social support, academic press, and student achievement: A view from the middle grades in Chicago.* A Report of the Chicago Annenberg Research Project. Chicago, IL: Consortium on Chicago School Research.

Legters, N.E., McDill, E.L. & McPartland, J.M. (1993). Rising to the challenge: Emerging strategies for educating youth at risk. In U.S. Dept. of Education, Office of Research and Improvement, Educational reforms and students at risk: A review of the current state of the art. (Contract #RR1172011). Washington, DC: Author.

Legters, N., McDill, E., & McPartland, J. (1994). *Compensatory education: Traditional responses and current tensions.* Baltimore: Center for Research on Effective Schooling for Disadvantaged Students, Johns Hopkins University. Retrieved on August 15, 2010 from http://www2.ed.gov/pubs/EdReformStudies/EdReforms/chap7a.html.

Lewin, K., & Little, A. (2011). Access to education revisited: Equity, drop out and transitions to secondary school in South Asia and Sub-Saharan Africa. *International Journal of Educational Development, 31*, 333–337.

Lillard, A.S. (2005). *Montessori: The science behind the genius.* New York: Oxford University Press.

Lillard, A., & Else-Quest, N. (2006). The early years: Evaluating Montessori education. *Science,313*(5795), pp. 1893–1894. Retrieved on September 20, 2010 from http://www.sciencemag.org/cgi/reprint/313/5795/1893.pdf.

Lillard, P.P. (1996). *Montessori today: A comprehensive approach to education from birth to childhood.* New York: Schocken Books.

Lipsitz, J., Mizell, H., Jackson, A., & Meyer-Austin, L. (1997). What works in middle grades reform? *Phi Delta Kappan, 78*(7), 517–519.

Lopata, C., Wallace, N., & Finn, K. (2005). Comparison of academic achievement between Montessori and traditional educational programs. *Journal of Research in Childhood Education, 20*(1), 5–13.

Loveless, T. (1999). *Tracking wars: State reform meets school policy.* Washington, DC: Brookings Institution Press.

MacIver, D., & Balfanz, R. (1999). *The school district's role in helping high-poverty schools become high-performing.* In including at-risk students in standards-based reform: A report on McRel's diversity roundtable II. Aurora, CO: Mid-Continent Research for Education and Learning.

MacIver, M., & Farley, E. (2003). *Bringing the district back in: The role of Central Office in improving instruction and student achievement* (CRESPAR Report #65). Baltimore, MD and Washington, DC: Center for Research on the Education of Students Placed at Risk.

Mallady, S.V. (2009). China seeks state expertise on Activity-Based Learning method. *The Hindu*, November 16, 2009. Retrieved on March 17, 2010 from http://www.thehindu.com/news/states/tamil-nadu/article49381.ece.

Marsh, J.A. (2000). *Connecting districts to the policy dialogue: A review of literature on the relationship of districts with states, schools and communities.* Seattle, WA: Center for the Study of Teaching and Policy, University of Washington.

Massell, D. (2000). *The district role in building capacity: Four strategies.* CPRE Policy Briefs, RB-32.

Math and Science Partnership Network. (n.d.). *Math and science partnership: Program impact report.* Washington D.C.: National Science Foundation. Retrieved on July 1, 2012 from http://www.nsf.gov/news/newsmedia/msp_impact/msp_exec_summary.pdf

———. (n.d). *Puerto Rico MSP profile.* Retrieved on July 1, 2012 from http://puertorico.mspnet.org/index.cfm/profile.

McDonald, K., Wilson, L., & Jack, A. (n.d.). *Public social partnerships in Scotland: Lessons learned.* Edinburgh, Scotland: Forth Sector. Retrieved on

July 12, 2012 from http://www.socialfirms.org.uk/FileLibrary/Resources/ Procurement/PSP%20LessonsLearned%20-%20full.pdf.

Middle Start National Center (2007). *Middle Start evidence of effectiveness.* New York: Academy for Educational Development.

———. (n.d.). *What we do.* New York: Academy for Educational Development. Retrieved from http://middlestart.org/what-we-do/on August, 12, 2010.

Miller, L.B., & Bizzell, R.P. (1984). Long term effects of four pre-school programs; ninth and tenth grade results. *Child Development, 55* (4), 1570–1588.

Ministry of Education—Pakistan. (2009). *National education policy 2009.* Islamabad, Pakistan: Ministry of Education.

Ministry of Education—Singapore. (2012). *Compulsory education.* Singapore: Ministry of Education. Retrieved from http://www.moe.gov.sg/initiatives/ compulsory-education/on June 19, 2012.

Ministry of Human Resource Development. (n.d.). *Sarva Shiksha Abhiyan.* Retrieved from http://www.ssa.nic.in on June 19, 2012.

Molnar,A., & Garcia, D.R. (2007). The expanding role of privatization in education: Implications for teacher education and development. *Teacher Education Quarterly, 34*(2): 11–24.

Montessori, M. (1967/1995). *The absorbent mind.* New York: Henry Holt and Co. Translated by Claude Claremont.

Mooney, C. (2005). *Theories of childhood: An introduction to Dewey, Montessori, Erikson, Piaget and Vygotsky.* St. Paul, MN: Red Leaf Press.

National Alliance for Public Charter Schools. (2010). *Measuring charter performance: A review of public charter school achievement studies* (Sixth edition). Washington, DC: National Alliance for Public Charter Schools.

National Forum to Accelerate Middle-Grades Reform. (n.d.). *Vision statement.* Savoy, IL: National Forum to Accelerate Middle-Grades Reform. Retrieved on March 13, 2011 from http://www.middlegradesforum.org/index.php/ about/vision-mission.

National Research Council. (2002). *Scientific research in education.* Washington, DC: The National Academies Press.

National Science Foundation. (2010). *National impact report.* Washington, DC: National Science Foundation. Retrieved on June 7, 2012 from http://www. nsf.gov/pubs/2010/nsf10046/nsf10046.pdf.

National Staff Development Council. (n.d.). *Proposed amendments to Section 9101 (34) of the Elementary and Secondary Education Act as reauthorized by the No Child Left Behind Act of 2001.* Oxford, OH: National Staff Development Council. Retrieved on June 22, 2011 from http://www.nsdc. org/standfor/definition.cfm.

Narayan, V. (2010). The private and the public in school education. *Economic and Political Weekly, XLV*(6), 23–26, February 6, 2010.

Neufeld, B., & Roper, D. (2003). *Coaching: A strategy for developing instructional capacity.* Washington, DC: Aspen Institute Program on Education and Providence.

Oakes, J. (1986). *Keeping track: How schools structure inequality.* New Haven: Yale University Press.

————. (2008). *Beyond tracking: Multiple pathways to college, career, and civic participation.* Cambridge, MA: Harvard University Press.

Ochs, K. (2009). *Praxis: European venture philanthropy in practice.* Brussels, Belgium: European Venture Philanthropy Association.

OECD—Organization for Economic Co-operation and Development. (2010). *Shanghai and Hong Kong: Two distinct examples of education reform in China.* Paris: OECD.

————. (2012). *Public and private schools: How management and funding relate to their socio-economic profile.* Paris: OECD Publishing. Retrieved from http://dx.doi.org/10.1787/9789264175006-en on July 1, 2012.

Piaget, J. (1967/1971). Biology and knowledge: An essay on the relation between organic regulations and cognitive processes. Chicago: University of Chicago Press.

Polakow, V. (1992). *The erosion of childhood.* Chicago, IL: University of Chicago Press.

Patrinos, H., & Sosale, S. (2007). *Mobilizing the private sector for public education: A view from the trenches.* Washington, DC: The World Bank.

Pratham. (n.d.). *ASER.* New Delhi: Pratham. Retrieved on May 7, 2009 from http://www.pratham.org/M-19-3-ASER.aspx.

Raghupathi, H. (2009). *Tamil Nadu: A tale of two reports.* Education World, April 6, 2009. Retrieved on May 9, 2010 from http://www.educationworldonline.net/index.php/page-article-choice-more-id-1683

Ramalingam, A. (2012). Corporation schools to have Montessori environments. *Times of India,* May 13, 2012. Retrieved on July 5, 2012 from http://articles.timesofindia.indiatimes.com/2012-05-13/chennai/31689575_1_montessori-education-corporation-schools-kindergarten-sections.

Ramirez, H. (2007). *Los Angeles takes over its school district: An overview of Mayor Antonio Villaraigosa's bid to restructure LAUSD.* Los Angeles, CA: Tomas Rivera Policy Institute, University of Southern California.

Rothstein, J. (2007). Does competition among public schools benefit students and taxpayers? A comment on Hoxby (2000). *American Economic Review, 97*(5), 2026–2037.

Sankaranarayanan, A. (2012). Beyond the right to education lies a school of hard knocks. Opinion, *The Hindu,* April 17, 2012.

Sarangapani, P.M., & Winch, W. (2010). Tooley, Dixon and Gomathi on private education in Hyderabad: A reply. *Oxford Review of Education, 36*(4), 499–515.

Sarva Shiksha Abhiyan. (n.d). *Activity Based Learning.* Tamil Nadu: Sarva Shiksha Abhiyan. Retrieved on October 2, 2010 from http://www.ssa.tn.nic.in/CurrActivities-A.htm/

————. (n.d.). *Annual work plan and budget: Quality initiatives and issues and strategies.* Tamil Nadu: Sarva Shiksha Abhiyan. Retrieved on May 7, 2009 from http://www.ssa.tn.nic.in/Docu/Chapter%20III.pdf.

Sarva Shiksha Abhiyan. (2010). *In-service teacher training.* Tamil Nadu: Sarva Shiksha Abhiyan. Retrieved from http://www.ssa.tn.nic.in/Docu/Training%202009-10.pdf on March 17, 2010.

Sarva Shiksha Abhiyan & Krishnamurthi Foundation of India. (2008). *Active learning methodology.* Tamil Nadu: Sarva Shiksha Abhiyan.

Schoolscape Center for Educators. (2009). *Activity-based learning: Effectiveness of ABL under SSA.* Chennai: Schoolscape Center for Educators.

Scottish Government. (2011). *A practical guide to forming and operating public social partnerships.* Edinburgh, Scotland: The Scottish Government. Retrieved on July 12, 2012 from http://www.scotland.gov.uk/Topics/People/15300/enterprising-organisation/PSPGuidance2011.

Simmons, W., Foley, E., & Ucelli, M. (2006). Using mayoral involvement in district reform to support instructional change. *Harvard Education Review, 76*(2,Summer), 147–152.

Sims, C. (2010). *A review of research on the 'Teach for' programs based in the USA, UK, and other countries (Teach for All).* Queensland, Australia: Queensland College of Teachers.

Slavin, R.E., & Fashola, O. (1998). *Show me the evidence!* Thousand Oaks, CA: Corwin.

Smith, D.R. (2005). Eggman and the empress. *Montessori Life, 17* (3, Summer), 50–54.

Spillane, J.P., & C.L. Thompson (1997). Reconstructing conceptions of local capacity: The local education agency's capacity for ambitious instructional reform. *Education Evaluation and Policy Analysis, 19*(2), 185–203.

Spillane, J.P., (2000). *District leaders' perception of teacher learning.* CPRE Occasional Paper Series OP-05. Philadelphia, PA: Center for Policy Research in Education.

————. (2006). *The case for district-based reform: Leading, building, and sustaining school improvement.* Cambridge, MA: Harvard University Press.

Srinivasan, M. (2008). Passionate about education. *The Hindu*, July 27, 2008. Retrieved on September 13, 2010 from http://www.hindu.com/2008/07/27/stories/2008072757510200.htm.

Stone, C.N., Henig, J.R., Jones, B.D., & Pierannunzi, C. (2001). *Building civic capacity: The politics of reforming urban schools.* Lawrence, KS: University Press of Kansas.

Stringfield, S., & Datnow, A. (1998). Introduction: Scaling up school restructuring designs in urban schools. *Education and Urban Society, 30*(3), 269–276.

The Hindu. (2009). Primary education system in Chennai found worth emulation. *The Hindu*, March 3, 2009. Retrieved on March 17, 2010 from http://www.hindu.com/2009/03/03/stories/2009030354660600.htm.

————. (2009). Corporation teachers get diploma in Montessori. *The Hindu*, November 18, 2009. Retrieved on July 5, 2012 from http://www.hindu.com/2009/11/18/stories/2009111850280200.htm.

Tilak, J.B. (2010). Public-private partnership in education. *The Hindu*, Opinion, May 25, 2010. Retrieved from http://www.thehindu.com/opinion/lead/article437492.ece on July 16, 2011.

Times of India. (2012). Right to education free admissions: Top CBSE schools get mild response on day one. Times of India, June 21, 2012. Retrieved on July 12, 2012 from http://articles.timesofindia.indiatimes.com/2012-06-21/nagpur/32351349_1_cbse-schools-top-cbse-applicants.

Toch, T. (1999). Whittling away the public school monopoly. *The Wall Street Journal.* November 15, 1999. Retrieved from http://www.brookings.edu/research/opinions/1999/11/15education-toch.

Tomlinson, C.A. (2000a). *The differentiated classroom: Responding to the needs of all learners.* Alexandria: Association for Supervision and Curriculum Development.

———. (2000b). Reconciliable differences. *Educational Leadership 58*(1), 6–11.

Tomlinson, A., Brimjoin, K., & L. Narvaez. (2008). *Differentiated school: Making revolutionary changes in teaching and learning.* Alexandria, VA: Association for Supervision and Curriculum Development.

Tooley, J. (2009). *The beautiful tree: A personal journey into how the world's poorest people are educating themselves.* New Delhi: Penguin; Washington, DC: Cato Institute.

Tooley, J., Dixon, P., & Gomathi, S.V. (2007). Private schools and the millennium development goal of universal primary education: A census and comparative survey in Hyderabad, India, in Hyderabad, India. *Oxford Review of Education, 33*(5), 539–560.

Travers, E. (2003). Philadelphia school reform: Historical roots and reflections on the 2002-2003 school year under state takeover. *Penn GSE Perspectives on Urban Education, 2*(2, Fall 2003), 18. Retrieved on July 1, 2012 from http://www.urbanedjournal.org/archive/volume-2-issue-2-fall-2003/philadelphia-school-reform-historical-roots-and-reflections-2002-

Tushnet, N., & Harris, D. (2006). The influence of states and districts on comprehensive school reform. In D.A. Borman (Ed.), *Examining comprehensive school reform* (pp. 57–80). Washington, DC: The Urban Institute Press.

Tyack, D., & Cuban, L. (1995). *Tinkering toward utopia: A century of public school reform.* Cambridge, MA: Harvard University Press.

UNESCO—United Nations Education, Scientific, and Cultural Organization. (2010). *Education for all global monitoring report: Reaching the marginalized.* Paris: UNESCO.

United States Department of Education. (2000). No Child Left Behind Act, Title I, Part F, Section 1606. Retrieved on June 22, 2011 from http://www2.ed.gov/policy/elsec/leg/esea02/pg13.html.

Vanek, W. (2001). *A new type of cooperative: Some historical background.* Stillwater, PA: Grassroots Economic Organizing.

Vygotsky, L.S. (1962). *Thought and language.* Cambridge, MA: MIT Press (Original work published in 1934).

Woessmann, L. (2006). *Public-private partnerships and schooling outcomes across countries.* CESifo Working Paper no. 1662, February. Munich: CESifo Group.

Wong, K.K., & Shen, F.X. (2003). Measuring the effectiveness of city and state takeover as a school reform strategy. *Peabody Journal of Education, 78*(4), 89–119.

World Bank. (n.d.). *Field visit to Sarva Shiksha Abhiyan in Tamil Nadu: Back to office report.* Washington D.C.: World Bank. Retrieved on June 24, 2012 from http://www.ssa.tn.nic.in/Docu/World_Bank_Team%20_Report.pdf.

World Development Report. (2004). *Making services work for poor people.* Washington, DC: World Bank.

Index

About the Author

Pritha Gopalan is an educational anthropologist engaged in research on public education reform. She has conducted extensive ethnographic research on social and educational issues in India and the United States over the last 20 years. She currently teaches at the Department of Humanities and Social Sciences at the Indian Institute of Technology, Madras, and previously worked at the Institute for Financial and Managerial Research, Chennai, and at the Academy for Educational Development, New York. Dr. Gopalan received her Ph.D. from the Graduate School of Education at the University of Pennsylvania.